RING
A
RING
O'ROSES

RING A RING O'ROSES

The Origins and Meanings of Old Rhymes

DIANA FERGUSON

Michael O'Mara Books Limited

First published in Great Britain in 2018 by
Michael O'Mara Books Limited
9 Lion Yard
Tremadoc Road
London SW4 7NQ

A CIP catalogue record for this book is available from the British Library.

Papers used by Michael O'Mara Books Limited are natural,
recyclable products made from wood grown in sustainable
forests. The manufacturing processes conform to the
environmental regulations of the country of origin.

ISBN: 978-1-78243-988-2 in hardback print format
ISBN: 978-1-78243-990-5 in ebook format

1 2 3 4 5 6 7 8 9 10

www.mombooks.com

Cover design by Ana Bjezancevic
Designed by Tetragon, London
Typeset by Kay Hayden

Image credits: Clipart.com: pages 44, 59, 66, 70, 108, 113, 123, 144;
iStock: page 28; Shutterstock: pages 33, 46, 80, 98, 114, 119, 165, 171, 176.

Every reasonable effort has been made to acknowledge all
copyright holders. Any errors or omissions that may have
occurred are inadvertent, and anyone with any copyright queries
is invited to write to the publisher, so that full acknowledgement
may be included in subsequent editions of the work.

Printed and bound by CPI Group (UK) Ltd, Croydon, CR0 4YY

CONTENTS

INTRODUCTION

STEP INTO THE world of nursery rhymes and you enter an Alice-in-Wonderland realm that makes little sense, where mice weave, birds weep, cows jump over the moon and where, for some unfathomable reason, old women head aloft in airborne baskets to sweep cobwebs off the sky. There are hundreds of nursery rhymes – far more than can be fitted into the pages of this book – and some are better known than others. I have attempted to present the more familiar ones here, inasmuch as space will allow.

Apart from a few exceptions, most nursery rhymes have no identifiable author or known provenance and may go back centuries. Like folk songs, they are an organic form and belong to the oral tradition. Even those that do have authors have become so well known that they, too, are now part of oral memory: the writers' names are long forgotten but the words remain. This seems to be one of the criteria that separates nursery rhymes from poems. Poems have the poet's stamp of ownership on them; nursery rhymes belong to no one and everyone.

With their roots in folk tradition, some rhymes began life as song lyrics or were associated with dances or singing games – indeed many still have their own accompanying tunes. The more familiar rhymes first made it onto the printed page in chapbooks: small, cheaply produced pamphlets that were sold by street hawkers ('chapman' is an old English name for a trader). Appearing in the sixteenth century and becoming more widespread in the seventeenth and eighteenth centuries, they featured all kinds of popular material, such as folk tales, ballads, poems and political tracts, often accompanied by illustrations.

Then, in the eighteenth and nineteenth centuries, nursery rhymes moved up in the world – and firmly into the nursery – when serious collectors began recording and publishing them. Among the various anthologies, certain key books stand out as significant early sources of rhymes. Published in 1744, *Tommy Thumb's Pretty Song Book*, the work of an anonymous author, is the earliest surviving collection of English nursery rhymes. In about 1765, *Mother Goose's Melody: or, Sonnets for the Cradle* made its appearance, published, it is believed, by the English publisher John Newbery. This was followed in 1784 by *Gammer Gurton's Garland, or, The Nursery Parnassus*, collated by the English antiquarian Joseph Ritson, while nearly a century later, in 1842, the scholar and antiquarian James Orchard Halliwell published his notable *The Nursery Rhymes of England*.

Occasionally these collectors offered background information to the rhymes, but often only the verses themselves were presented.

Attempts to interpret particular nursery rhymes have taxed many a brain over the centuries. While some of the theories are alluring, much of what has been proposed remains speculation. But the rhymes are a fascinating slice of social history, offering us a glimpse into the vanished world in which they arose, before industrialization, mass production or the introduction of a systematized welfare system to help the poor. The setting for many of the rhymes is similarly (and nostalgically) archaic – it's the farm or the village or the small town, where you might work as a shepherd or a cobbler or a candle-maker.

In a world without the scientific and practical support systems we now enjoy, life must have seemed a precarious experience, so it's only natural that people were superstitious and on the lookout for signs of what was to come – whether good or bad – and this is reflected in some of the rhymes. Nature, a force that humans could not control, was a prime source of such portents. A ladybird, for example, could bring good luck whereas sightings of magpies, depending on the number, could augur well or ill. Tantalizingly distant, the moon and stars exerted special magical powers. The day of the week on which a child was born was indicative of their fortune, while praying to the saints at bedtime would help to see you safely through the night.

Nursery rhymes have provided fodder for literature too. Beatrix Potter, for example, quoted particular rhymes in several of her books, and even used them as inspiration for plots. The combination of innocence (the recipients are little children) and ambiguity (the often bizarre content of some verses) can give the rhymes a sinister edge. This was not lost on certain writers, most notably the queen of crime detection, Agatha Christie, who based not only the titles but also the plotlines of some of her works on certain rhymes, for example: *One, Two, Buckle My Shoe* (1940), *Five Little Pigs* (1941), *Crooked House* (1949), *A Pocket Full of Rye* (1953), *Hickory Dickory Dock* (1955) and *Three Blind Mice* (1950), which would later become the long-running play *The Mousetrap*. In her 1941 spy thriller *N or M?*, *Goosey Goosey Gander* is the title of a book of nursery rhymes that contained, in invisible ink, the names of all the Nazi spies in England.

Dating back centuries in oral tradition and five hundred or more years since they began their move into print, these age-old rhymes continue to entertain new generations of children. Let us hope that this rich repository of cultural heritage will be remembered, treasured and enjoyed by many more generations to come.

CHAPTER 1

ANIMAL ANTICS

IN THIS NURSERY menagerie cats, mice, birds and the odd pig and invertebrate get up to all sorts of unlikely tricks – they shin up clocks, weave cloth, play the fiddle, jump over the moon, make royal visits and attend the funeral of one of their own.

Mice

Hickory, Dickory, Dock

> Hickory, dickory, dock,
> The mouse ran up the clock.
> The clock struck one,
> The mouse ran down,
> Hickory, dickory, dock.

This rhyme first appeared in print as 'Hichere, Dickere Dock' in *Tommy Thumb's Pretty Song Book*, in 1744. It is said to have been used by children as a counting-down rhyme to decide who should start a game – rather like 'Eeny, Meeny, Miney, Mo' (see page 174). The first and last lines may give a clue to its

AGATHA CHRISTIE'S BLIND MICE

As mentioned earlier, the famous crime writer Agatha Christie, recognizing the sinister undertones of some nursery rhymes, often made use of them in her stories. In 1947, the BBC broadcast Christie's radio play *Three Blind Mice*. The whodunit tells the story of the residents of a guesthouse who find themselves snowed in and trapped with a murderer. Christie later turned the script into a short story, which in turn was adapted as a stage play. Renamed *The Mousetrap*, it was first performed in London's West End in 1952. More than sixty years later, it is still going, making it the longest-running West End show ever.

possible origins in the archaic numbering system used by Westmoreland shepherds to count their sheep: *hevera*, for eight, *devera*, for nine, and *dick*, for ten.

An alternative suggestion is that it was intended to mock Richard Cromwell (1626–1712), who succeeded his father Oliver Cromwell as Lord Protector of the Commonwealth of England,

Scotland and Ireland. An ineffectual leader, Richard was derided with nicknames such as Tumbledown Dick and Hickory Dick. By the time the metaphorical clocks had rung out the end of his first year in power, he had been forced out of office.

Six Little Mice Sat Down to Spin

Six little mice sat down to spin;
Pussy passed by and she peeped in.
What are you doing, my little men?
Weaving coats for gentlemen.
Shall I come in and cut off your threads?
No, no, Mistress Pussy, you'd bite off our heads.
Oh, no, I'll not; I'll help you to spin.
That may be so, but you don't come in.

First printed in about 1840, in *Nursery Rhymes from the Royal Collection*s, this rhyme varies in the number of mice mentioned – sometimes there are only three, sometimes as many as ten. But however many there are, the age-old enmity between cat and mouse remains the same.

BEATRIX POTTER'S MICE

The fourth line of this rhyme is credited as inspiring Beatrix Potter to write *The Tailor of Gloucester*, published in 1903. The author often used nursery rhymes as a starting point for narrative sequences of drawings. In 1892, she began work on six watercolours illustrating the first six lines of the version that's titled 'Three Little Mice Sat Down to Spin', which she hoped could be made into a booklet. Although the booklet never materialized, the watercolour depicting the fourth line, 'Making coats for Gentlemen', was adapted for the 1903 book, which also drew on the true story of a real Gloucester tailor, John Pritchard. The rhyme itself makes its way into the text, when used by the mice to taunt the tailor's cat Simpkin who is scratching to be let in to eat them up. Potter's original watercolour of the industrious mice is now housed in the Victoria and Albert Museum in London.

Three Blind Mice, Three Blind Mice

Three blind mice, three blind mice,
See how they run, see how they run!
They all ran after the farmer's wife,
Who cut off their tails with a carving knife,
Did you ever see such a thing in your life,
As three blind mice?

One of those singing rhymes that also has a familiar tune, this belongs to a category of song called a 'round' or 'roundelay': a short, simple song with a repetitive refrain. The term derives from the Old French word *rond*, meaning a circle, and 'lay', a poem to be sung.

It does not seem to have made its way into the nursery until 1842, when it appeared in James Orchard Halliwell's *The Nursery Rhymes of England*. The rhyme itself, however, dates back much further than this. In 1609, an early version was included among the 'Pleasant Roundelaies' in *Deuteromelia, or, The Seconde part of Musicks melodie*, collected and partly written by Thomas Ravenscroft:

Three blinde Mice, three blinde Mice,
Dame Iulian, Dame Iulian,
the Miller and his merry olde Wife,
shee scrapte her tripe licke thou the knife.

Birds

Goosey, Goosey Gander

Goosey, goosey gander,
Whither shall I wander?
Upstairs and downstairs
And in my lady's chamber.
There I met an old man
Who would not say his prayers.
I took him by the left leg
And threw him down the stairs.

Another nursery rhyme that makes little logical sense but tantalizes us into trying to unpick just what is going on here.

- One suggestion is that it refers to the hiding places known as 'priest holes' that Catholic priests used during the persecution of Catholics by Henry VIII and later Oliver Cromwell. If discovered and 'unable to say his prayers' – Protestant prayers, that is – the priest would be forcibly dragged out.
- The word 'goose' has long had sexual associations and was once used as a synonym for prostitute. Has an old man been caught 'in my lady's chamber' with such a woman?

The oldest-known recorded version of this rhyme appeared in 1784, in *Gammer Gurton's Garland, or, The Nursery Parnassus*:

> Goose-a, goose-a, gander,
> Where shall I wander?
> Up stairs, down stairs,
> In my lady's chamber;
> There you'll find a cup of sack
> And a race of ginger.

This version has only two concluding lines, which are unlike the final four that we know now, so it is possible that the latter were taken from a different rhyme to replace the former. They closely resemble a traditional rhyme addressed to the crane-fly, or 'Daddy Long-legs', as first printed in *Nancy Cock's Pretty Song Book for all Little Misses and Masters* in 1780:

> Old father Long-Legs
> Can't say his prayers:
> Take him by the left leg,
> And throw him downstairs.

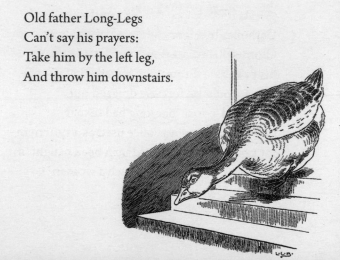

Two Little Dicky Birds

> Two little dicky birds,
> Sitting on a wall;
> One named Peter,
> The other named Paul.
> Fly away, Peter!
> Fly away, Paul!
> Come back, Peter!
> Come back, Paul!

An 'action rhyme' with which adults have bamboozled young children for decades, thus:

1. Tear off two small pieces of paper, dampen them to make them sticky, and press one onto each index finger, one for 'Peter', one for 'Paul'.

2. Place both index fingers on a flat surface: the little pieces of paper are the two little dicky birds sitting on the wall.

3. Start reciting the rhyme, wiggling each index finger in turn to draw attention to Peter and to Paul.

4. When you get to 'Fly away, Peter! Fly away, Paul!', whip your hands away, then bring them back with the index fingers tucked out of sight and your middle fingers showing instead – the birds have 'flown away'.

5. Reverse the process to bring back Peter and Paul.

An older version of the rhyme, recorded in *Mother Goose's Melody: or, Sonnets for the Cradle*, from around 1765, cites blackbirds instead, with the generic names Jack and Jill. But it seems likely that these were replaced with those of Christ's two chief apostles in more pious Victorian times.

Who Killed Cock Robin?

Who killed Cock Robin?
I, said the Sparrow,
With my bow and arrow,
I killed Cock Robin.

Who saw him die?
I, said the Fly,
With my little eye,
I saw him die.

Who caught his blood?
I, said the Fish,
With my little dish,
I caught his blood.

Who'll make the shroud?
I, said the Beetle,

With my thread and needle,
I'll make the shroud.

Who'll dig his grave?
I, said the Owl,
With my pick and shovel,
I'll dig his grave.

Who'll be the parson?
I, said the Rook,
With my little book,
I'll be the parson.

Who'll be the clerk?
I, said the Lark,
If it's not in the dark,
I'll be the clerk.

Who'll carry the link?
I, said the Linnet,
I'll fetch it in a minute,
I'll carry the link.

Who'll be the chief mourner?
I, said the Dove,
I mourn for my love,
I'll be the chief mourner.

Who'll carry the coffin?
I, said the Kite,

If it's not through the night,
I'll carry the coffin.

Who'll bear the pall?
We, said the Wren,
Both the cock and the hen,
We'll bear the pall.

Who'll sing a psalm?
I, said the Thrush,
As she sat on a bush,
I'll sing a psalm.

Who'll toll the bell?
I, said the Bull,
Because I can pull,
I'll toll the bell.

All the birds of the air
Fell a-sighing and a-sobbing,
When they heard the bell toll
For poor Cock Robin.

The more you read this rhyme, the more sinister it sounds. With its hypnotic rhythm, it has the quality of an incantation – of some ritualistic chant in which 'all the birds of the air' collude in the murder and burial of poor Cock Robin.

The opening four verses were first printed in 1744, in *Tommy Thumb's Pretty Song Book*, but there has been much speculation that the verses are considerably older and express a more universal theme:

- Versions of the rhyme exist in other European countries, such as Germany, which suggests that they have a common cultural root. One theory cites the myth of the murder of Balder, Norse god of light.
- In a similar vein, in Celtic tradition, the story of Cock Robin's death may allude to the passing of *coch rhi-ben*, or 'red chief king', a possible common name for the Celtic solar god Lugh, whose radiant face glowed red like the sun. Lugh ruled over the summer half of the year but was supplanted by the 'sparrow' of the god Bran – the wren, in the rhyme – who rules winter.
- In the fifth verse, 'owl' is rhymed with 'shovel'. This suggests that the original word here was 'shouell', 'shoul' or 'showl', which is fourteenth-century Old English: another clue to its antiquity.
- Archaeologists have pointed out that a fifteenth-century stained-glass window at Buckland Rectory in Gloucester shows a bird, with the markings of a robin, pierced through the breast with an arrow.
- The 'bull' referred to in the rhyme is not a farmyard animal, but a bullfinch.

Cats

Ding, Dong, Bell

Ding, dong, bell,
Pussy's in the well.
Who put her in?
Little Johnny Green.
Who pulled her out?
Little Tommy Stout.
What a naughty boy was that,
To try to drown poor pussy cat,
Who never did him any harm,
And killed the mice in his father's barn.

Although in different forms, this rhyme goes back at least five centuries; John Lant, an organist at Winchester Cathedral, recorded the following version in 1580:

Jacke boy, ho boy newes,
the cat is in the well,
let us ring now for her Knell,
ding dong ding dong Bell.

This verse appeared again in 1609, in Thomas Ravenscroft's *Pammelia, Musicks Miscellanie*, as a song for four voices. Shakespeare also used the refrain 'ding dong bell' in more than one of his plays; for example, in 'Ariel's Song' in *The Tempest*, and in *The Merchant of Venice*.

A form that resembles the more familiar rhyme was first published in about 1765, in *Mother Goose's Melody: or, Sonnets for the Cradle*. In 1949, a kinder adaptation of the rhyme was offered in Geoffrey Hall's *New Nursery Rhymes for Old*, in which Pussy is only 'at' the well, not 'in' it.

✼ ❋ ✼

Hey Diddle Diddle

Hey diddle diddle,
The cat and the fiddle,
The cow jumped over the moon;
The little dog laughed
To see such sport,
And the dish ran away with the spoon.

A number of wild and unproven theories have been put forward regarding the origins and meaning of this piece – for example, that it is connected with worship of the Egyptian cow goddess Hathor or that it refers to Katherine of Aragon (Katherine la Fidèle). All that can be said for sure is that it is perhaps the best-known English nonsense rhyme, and that it was first printed in *Mother Goose's Melody*. This *c.* 1765 version reads:

High diddle, diddle,
The Cat and the Fiddle,
The Cow jump'd over the Moon;
The little Dog laugh'd to see such Craft,
And the Dish ran away with the Spoon.

In other, later versions, a maid – not a dish – runs away with the spoon, and athletic goats rather than a cow launch themselves skyward to vault over the moon.

Pussy Cat, Pussy Cat, Where Have You Been?

Pussy cat, pussy cat, where have you been?
I've been to London to look at the queen,
Pussy cat, pussy cat, what did you there?
I frightened a little mouse under her chair.

The queen here is usually thought to have been Elizabeth I. Tradition has it that a dozing cat was actually startled under her 'chair', or throne, and was pardoned by the Queen on condition that it kept the palace free of rats and mice.

Little children have often taken the rhyme as literal fact related to whichever queen is on the throne at the time:

- When invited by Queen Victoria to Osborne House, the royal residence on the Isle of Wight, British aristocrat and politician Lord Ernle relayed a message from his daughter: she wanted the Queen to give her 'the little mouse that lives under the chair'. Victoria was delighted and explained the little girl's request by reciting the rhyme to the assembled guests.
- In 1949, when Elizabeth, the Queen Mother, was visiting a Royal Air Force station, a little boy indignantly asked her where her pussy cat was; the Queen apologized for not bringing it with her.

Three Little Kittens They Lost Their Mittens

Three little kittens they lost their mittens,
And they began to cry,
Oh, mother dear, we sadly fear
That we have lost our mittens.
What! lost your mittens, you naughty kittens!
Then you shall have no pie.
Mee-ow, mee-ow, mee-ow.
No, you shall have no pie.

The three little kittens they found their mittens,
And they began to cry,
Oh, mother dear, see here, see here,
For we have found our mittens.
Put on your mittens, you silly kittens,
And you shall have some pie.
Purr-r, purr-r, purr-r,
Oh, let us have some pie.

These 'naughty kittens' belong to the same camp as Beatrix Potter's Tom Kitten who cannot keep his clothes clean. Two further verses go on to describe how they soil their mittens while eating the pies, but then wash them and hang them out to dry.

The verses have been ascribed to Eliza Follen (1787–1860), a children's writer from New England. They appear in her *New Nursery Songs for All Good Children* but are described as 'traditional' so perhaps predate this publication.

Miscellaneous Animals

Ladybird, Ladybird

Ladybird, ladybird,
Fly away home,
Your house is on fire
And your children all gone;
All except one
And that's little Ann
And she has crept under
The warming pan.

MAGIC BEETLE

Numerous beliefs and superstitions are attached to the ladybird – it's considered unlucky to kill one, for example. In Scotland, where the seven-spot ladybird is known as King Calowa, you can ask the insect's help with your love life using this traditional rhyme:

King, King Calowa
Up your wings and flee awa'
Over land, and over sea;
Tell me where my love can be.

This is one of those fascinating rhymes that look innocent at first but have hidden depths. The traditional way to recite it is to place a real ladybird on your finger and address her directly. At the second line, you blow gently on the insect, who will almost always heed your warning, lift her wings and 'fly away home'.

What looks like a childish rhyme, however, is thought to be a relic of some ancient incantation. A German theory suggests that it was once a charm to help the sun across the red sky – namely, the 'house on fire' – at sunset. It has also been associated with the worship of the Egyptian goddess Isis and the Norse goddess Freya.

Similar rhymes are found in Denmark, France, Germany, Sweden and Switzerland, and the sacred status of this little beetle is revealed in the many names by which it is known; for example:

- Ladybird, from 'Our Lady's bird'; Marygold; or God's little cow (English)
- *Marienkäfer*, or Mary's beetle (German)
- *Marias Nyckelpiga*, or Mary's ladybird (Swedish)
- *Bête à bon Dieu*, or the Good Lord's beast (French)
- *Vaquilla de Dios*, or God's cow (Spanish)

This Little Piggy Went to Market

This little piggy went to market,
This little piggy stayed at home,
This little piggy had roast beef,
This little piggy had none,
And this little piggy cried, wee-wee-wee-wee-wee,
All the way home.

Like 'Two Little Dicky Birds' (see page 18), this is another action rhyme and counting game for toddlers and young children that involves tickling – and a lot of laughter. In the game, each of the child's toes represents one of the 'little piggies'.

1. 'This little piggy went to market': wiggle the big toe.

2. 'This little piggy stayed at home': wiggle the second toe.

3. 'This little piggy had roast beef': wiggle the third toe.

4. 'This little piggy had none': wiggle the fourth toe.

5. 'And this little piggy cried, wee-wee-wee-wee-wee, all the way home': wiggle the fifth, smallest toe and then tickle the child.

Children always know what's coming and wait in excited anticipation – then ask you to repeat the whole rhyme again.

The first-known full version was printed in *The Famous Tommy Thumb's Little Story-book* in about 1760. 'Piggy' dates from more recent times – it was originally 'pig'. For those of a vegetarian bent, an alternative 1890 version of the third line has the little piggy eating bread and butter rather than roast beef.

BEATRIX POTTER'S LITTLE PIGS

'Once upon a time there was an old pig called Aunt Pettitoes ...' So begins *The Tale of Pigling Bland* by that lover of nursery rhymes, Beatrix Potter. Finding a family of eight piglets too much to handle, the aunt sends Pigling and his brother Alexander off to market. On the way, Alexander sings:

'This pig went to market, this pig stayed at home,
This pig had a bit of meat—
let's see what they have given US for dinner, Pigling?'

CHAPTER 2

HAPLESS CHILDREN AND FOOLISH ADULTS

NURSERY RHYMES FAVOUR generic names for their characters, and among the Jacks, Marys, Toms and others, here are some of the most famous of all – the accident-prone Jack and Jill, the pet-obsessed Mary, the horticulturist Mary, the arachnophobic Miss Muffet … and, of course, the fatally injured figure we know only as 'Humpty Dumpty'.

Jack

I'll Tell You a Story

> I'll tell you a story
> About Jack a Nory,
> And now my story's begun;
> I'll tell you another
> Of Jack and his brother,
> And now my story is done.

First recorded in 1760, this rhyme offers the adult a way out when faced with persistent demands from children for yet another story. To vary the theme, you could always replace 'Jack a Nory' with some of the other names by which the character has been known:

1. Mother Morey (*c.* 1825)

2. Peg Amo-re (*c.* 1840)

3. Jack a Manory (1865)

4. Jacopo Minore (1890)

5. Jack a minory (1913)

6. Jock o'Binnorie (used by the poet Robert Graves in a poem of the same name).

Jack and Jill Went Up the Hill

Jack and Jill went up the hill
To fetch a pail of water;
Jack fell down and broke his crown,
And Jill came tumbling after.

Up Jack got, and home did trot,
As fast as he could caper,
To old Dame Dob, who patched his nob
With vinegar and brown paper.

Only the first verse of this nursery rhyme appears in the earliest printed version, *c.* 1765, in *Mother Goose's Melody*. The rhyming of 'water' with 'after' is archaic early seventeenth-century pronunciation, suggesting that the verse may be at least a century older.

The second verse probably dates from the nineteenth century, when the rhyme was extended to fifteen verses. The curious (to us) remedy for Jack's injury – vinegar and brown paper – was an old home cure to draw out bruises.

For such a well-known rhyme, its roots remain elusive and there have been various guesses as to its origins, such as:

- It is a metaphor alluding to characters in Norse myth – Hjuki, recast as 'Jack', and Bil, recast as 'Jill' – according to the English antiquarian, the Rev. Sabine Baring-Gould (1834–1924).
- It contains traces of some ancient mystic ceremony, according to the Scottish folklorist Lewis Spence (1874–1955). Spence argued that no one would climb to the top of a hill to collect water unless it was water with mystical properties, such as dew.
- It refers to the attempt by King Charles I to reduce the volume of the jack, an imperial liquid unit used to measure out alcohol, while

still levying the same amount of tax on it as before. By extension, a gill – double the size of a jack – would also 'come tumbling down'. The 1765 woodcut illustration to the first verse does show two boys, not a boy and a girl, described as 'Jack and Gill'. The phrase 'broke his crown' could also refer to the loss of the king's crown when Charles I was beheaded in 1649.

BOY MEETS GIRL

Jack and Jill should not be read as personal names but rather as archaic generic terms for 'lad' and 'lass', particularly in a romantic context. In 1567–8, a play entitled *Jack and Jill* was performed at the court of Elizabeth I, and Shakespeare used the phrase twice: 'Jack shall have Jill', in *A Midsummer Night's Dream*; and 'Jack hath not Jill', in *Love's Labour's Lost*. There is also the proverb, 'A good Jack makes a good Jill.'

Jack Be Nimble

Jack be nimble,
Jack be quick,
Jack jump over
The candlestick.

It seems that there are no obscure metaphors to
unearth in this brief rhyme – what it describes is a
real activity practised in England for many centuries.
Jumping over a candle was both a sport and a means
of fortune telling: 'jumping the candle for luck'. A
lighted candle was placed on the floor and if the
flame did not go out when a person jumped over it,
they were assured of good luck in the coming year.
The verse was recorded in 1815, as an addition to
Gammer Gurton's Garland.

Little Jack Horner

Little Jack Horner
Sat in the corner,
Eating a Christmas pie;
He put in his thumb,
And pulled out a plum,
And said, What a good boy am I!

A familiar interpretation of this rhyme is that it refers to a Jack Horner who was steward to Richard Whiting, the last of the abbots of Glastonbury Abbey. During Henry VIII's campaign against the Catholic Church and his appropriation of monastic property and wealth between 1536 and 1541 – known as the Dissolution of the Monasteries – the abbot sent his steward to the king with a conciliatory Christmas gift: a pie containing the title deeds to twelve manors. On the way there, so the story goes, Jack Horner opened the pie and stole the deeds to the manor of Mells in Somerset.

This fanciful story may have a tiny grain of truth in it, although no theft was involved. Historical records show that a Thomas Horner bought the manor of Mells in 1543, following the dissolution of Glastonbury Abbey in 1539 – or, as John Leland, a historian in the service of Henry VIII, observed when he visited Mells: 'Now Mr Horner hath boute the lordship of the King.' This is confirmed by the original title deed, which bore Henry's seal.

An early version of the rhyme was included in 'Namby Pamby', a ballad poem and political satire written by the English poet and satirist Henry Carey in 1725 to mock the Whig politician and poet Ambrose Philips. Carey opposed the Whig leader, Robert Walpole, whom Philips had eulogized, among others, in one of his own grandiose and flowery odes.

Carey parodied Philips' writing style and the term 'namby pamby' came to be a descriptive term for anything weak and overly sentimental.

❦ ✳ ❧

Mary

Mary Had a Little Lamb

Mary had a little lamb,
Its fleece was white as snow;
And everywhere that Mary went
The lamb was sure to go.

It followed her to school one day,
That was against the rule;
It made the children laugh and play
To see a lamb at school.

And so the teacher turned it out,
But still it lingered near,
And waited patiently about
Till Mary did appear.

Why does the lamb love Mary so?
The eager children cry;
Why, Mary loves the lamb, you know,
The teacher did reply.

One of the few nursery rhymes with a known author, this was written by Mrs Sarah Hale of Boston, in 1830, or at least the last three verses were – other contenders have been put forward as the originators of the remaining verses:

- Mary Sawyer, later Mary Tyler, from Massachusetts, claimed to be the original 'Mary' because she had a pet lamb that she took to school one day. She said that John Roulstone, a young man visiting the school, then wrote the verses to describe the incident. Henry Ford, founder of the Ford Motor Company, who had a personal interest in American cultural heritage, believed her and collected two hundred documents to support her claim.
- Some theories propose that Roulstone wrote just the first verse and that the remaining three, which are less childish in tone, were added by Sarah Hale. But others maintain that Sarah Hale was the author of the entire poem; indeed, in a letter written not long before her death, she herself insisted that Roulstone had no hand in its composition.
- Across the ocean in Wales, Mary Hughes, the daughter of a Welsh sheep farmer, also claimed to be the real 'Mary'. One of the lambs that

she hand-reared followed her to school one day and, she asserted, caused such a stir that a Miss Burls, visiting from London, was inspired to pen the famous verses. However, this Mary wasn't born until 1842, twelve years after the first publication of the rhyme.

If proof were needed of this nursery rhyme's fame, Thomas Edison recited it for his first recording on his newly invented phonograph – later known as the gramophone or record player – in 1877.

MARY MEMORABILIA

A statue of Mary's Little Lamb stands in the town centre of Sterling, Massachusetts, where Mary Tyler lived. The Redstone School, built in 1798 and thought to be the place mentioned in the rhyme, can be seen in Sudbury, Massachusetts. It was bought by Henry Ford and relocated there as part of his project to establish Sudbury as a themed historical village.

Mary, Mary, Quite Contrary

> Mary, Mary, quite contrary,
> How does your garden grow?
> With silver bells and cockle shells,
> And pretty maids all in a row.

Silver bells? Cockle shells? Pretty maids? And just who is this contrary Mary? There are two chief contenders, both Catholic queens at a time when Protestantism was asserting itself, and one other intriguing suggestion:

MARY STUART, QUEEN OF SCOTS

This Catholic queen reigned over Scotland from 1542 to 1587 and was 'contrary' in several ways: she had grown up in France and married the heir to the French throne before being widowed; she was regarded by many Scottish Catholics as the rightful heir to the English throne, then occupied by her Protestant cousin, Elizabeth I; and she was embroiled in various plots and intrigues that ultimately resulted in her beheading by Elizabeth.

Here are some interpretations of the lines:

- 'How does your garden grow?': a sarcastic reference to the hapless Queen's aspirations to the English throne.

- 'Silver bells': the bells of Catholic cathedrals.
- 'Cockle shells': the emblems worn by Catholic pilgrims.
- 'Pretty maids all in a row': the Four Marys, the Queen's renowned ladies-in-waiting.

MARY TUDOR, 'BLOODY MARY'

This Mary was the daughter of Catherine of Aragon, Henry VIII's first wife, and older sister to the Protestant Elizabeth I, Henry's second child by Anne Boleyn. She was Queen of England from 1553 to 1558. Staunchly Catholic, this 'contrary Mary' tried to reverse the breakaway from Catholicism started by her father and set about the brutal persecution of Protestants: it earned her the nickname 'Bloody Mary'.

Various interpretations of the rhyme have been suggested:

- 'How does your garden grow?': a jibe related to Mary's childlessness; or the common belief, then, that England had become a vassal of Catholic Spain, the homeland of Mary's husband, Philip II; or a play on words, relating to Mary's chief minister, Stephen Gardiner.
- 'Silver bells': a nickname for thumbscrews.
- 'Cockle shells': a nickname for an instrument

of torture attached to the genitals.

- 'Pretty maids all in a row': Mary's miscarriages; or the 'rows' of Protestants she had executed; or the 'maiden', a device for beheading.

MARY, MOTHER OF JESUS

There has also been speculation that the rhyme refers to the Virgin Mary, with the 'garden' alluding to a convent, the bells and cockle shells to Catholic symbols, and the 'pretty maids' to rows of praying nuns.

All of these are fascinating ideas, but they can only remain guesswork as there is no evidence that the rhyme was known before the eighteenth century. It was first printed in 1744, in *Tommy Thumb's Pretty Song Book*.

DARK ROYAL SECRETS

Nancy Cock's Pretty Song Book for all Little Misses and Masters, dating from 1780, offers an alternative last line – 'Sing cuckolds all on a row'. Could this refer back to the troubled marriages of the two contrary queens?

43

Tom

Little Tommy Tucker

Little Tommy Tucker
Sings for his supper:
What shall we give him?
White bread and butter.
How shall he cut it
Without a knife?
How will he be married
Without a wife?

A few scraps of information exist that may throw some light on the origins of this rhyme. A Thomas Tucker was appointed 'Prince or Lorde of the Revells' at St John's College, Oxford, in 1607, and a 'Tom Tuck' appears in an epigram written by the seventeenth-century poet Robert Herrick: 'At post and paire, or slam, Tom Tuck would play This Christmas, but his want wherewith sayes nay.' 'Tom would eate meat, but wants a knife' appears in the lyrics to a 1620 ballad, 'An excellent new Medley'.

'Tommy Tucker' was also a generic name for 'orphan', so another possible interpretation is that this was a mocking jibe at those unfortunates who had neither mother nor father, and had to beg or literally 'sing for their supper', a proverbial phrase that goes back centuries.

'Little Tommy Tucker' was not recorded in print until 1744, in *Tommy Thumb's Pretty Song Book*, but only the first four lines were given.

Tom, Tom, the Piper's Son

Tom, Tom, the piper's son,
Stole a pig and away he run;
The pig was eat
And Tom was beat,
And Tom went howling down the street.

A printed version of this rhyme appeared as long ago as 1795, in a chapbook entitled *Tom the Piper's Son*. In a related but older and longer version, however, Tom isn't a thief but an accomplished piper whose playing is so irresistible that 'even the pigs on their hind legs would after him prance'. These pigs are clearly animals but the 'pig' in the more familiar rhyme was something altogether different – it was, in fact, a kind of pig-shaped pastry filled with currants, with two currant eyes. Such sweet treats were common in the eighteenth century and could easily be bought from street vendors.

STREET CRIES

The streets of towns and cities once rang to the cries of hawkers bearing baskets or pushing barrows filled with every conceivable item or service that anyone might want, from lavender, oranges and gingerbread to spoons, brooms and knife-grinding services. To advertise his or her wares, a 'pig' seller might cry:

A long tail'd Pig,
Or a short tail'd Pig,
Or a Pig without any tail,
A Boar Pig, or a Sow Pig,
Or a Pig with a curly tail.
Take hold of the Tail and eat off his head;
And then you'll be sure the Pig hog is dead.

Girls

Lucy Locket Lost Her Pocket

Lucy Locket lost her pocket,
Kitty Fisher found it;
Not a penny was there in it,
Only ribbon round it.

The nursery-rhyme collector James Orchard Halliwell first recorded this verse in 1842, in *The Nursery Rhymes of England*. Halliwell maintained that the two women mentioned were well-known courtesans during the reign of King Charles II (1630–85). It's an enticing theory but, sadly, no supporting evidence has been found. And other ideas as to the possible identity of the two ladies have them living a century later:

- Lucy Lockit is the name of a character in *The Beggar's Opera*, written by John Gay in 1728. Was Gay referring back to Halliwell's courtesan, or did he just choose a generic name?
- Catherine Marie Fischer (1741–67), a real-life courtesan, has a stronger case for being the prototype of 'Kitty Fisher', if only because she pops up in other verses and in paintings: there is an air called 'Kitty Fisher' in *Thomson's Country Dances*, from 1760, for example, and Sir Joshua Reynolds painted Catherine's portrait three times. At the height of her fame in 1759, she was one of the first celebrities to be famous for being famous.

'Pocket' is an archaic name for pouch or small bag. If Lucy's pocket was empty, perhaps it was because she had fallen on hard times, unlike the celebrated Kitty who found it. All we know for sure is that the verse was sung in nurseries in Britain and America in the early nineteenth century, to the tune of 'Yankee Doodle'.

Little Miss Muffet

Little Miss Muffet
Sat on a tuffet,
Eating her curds and whey;
Along came a spider,
Who sat down beside her
And frightened Miss Muffet away.

Among the best known of all nursery rhymes, this has even been depicted by the great Pre-Raphaelite painter John Everett Millais (1829–96). 'Miss Muffet' has been linked with Patience Muffet, the stepdaughter of the entomologist Dr Thomas Muffet (1533–1604), who was particularly fascinated by spiders. However, there is no clear evidence of a connection and the verse did not appear in print until two hundred years after Muffet's death, in *Songs for the Nursery* published in 1805.

Using the basic verse form, it isn't too difficult to produce variations on 'Miss Muffet' – all you need is a quick change of name and a suitable rhyming word. A number of very similar rhymes have been created this way, but it is not possible to say which was the original:

- Little Mary Ester / Sat upon a tester
- Little Miss Mopsey / Sat in the shopsey
- Little Alice Sander / Sat upon a cinder
- Little Polly Flinders / Sat among the cinders
- Little Poll Parrot / Sat in his garret
- Little Jack Horner / Sat in the corner (see page 36)

The curds and whey on which Miss Muffet was snacking were not dissimilar to cottage cheese, the curds being the lumps of soft cheese and the whey being the liquid that separates from the curd during the coagulation process.

Boys

Georgie Porgie, Pudding and Pie

Georgie Porgie, pudding and pie,
Kissed the girls and made them cry;
When the boys came out to play,
Georgie Porgie ran away.

With such a specific name as Georgie, surely this rhyme is about a specific person? A number of names have been put forward, including Charles II and George I. But the following two Georges are the strongest contenders:

GEORGE VILLIERS, DUKE OF BUCKINGHAM

Charming, handsome Villiers (1592–1628) rose from the minor nobility to become the favourite and, possibly, secret lover of King James I of England and Ireland (formerly James VI of Scotland). Although the king publicly railed against homosexuality, which was then illegal, he nevertheless referred to Villiers as 'my sweet child and wife' and nicknamed him 'Steenie' after St Stephen, who was said to have the 'face of an angel'. James conferred several titles on his favourite, culminating in 1623 with a dukedom.

If he really was James's lover, Villiers also had numerous liaisons with women and exploited the king's patronage to advance his own position of power. This made him hugely unpopular so that when, in 1628, he was stabbed to death in Portsmouth by an army officer, the public hailed his killer as a hero.

GEORGE IV

Born in 1762 and succeeding to the throne of Great Britain and Ireland in 1820, this George can lay an even stronger claim to the rhyme: he was grossly fat, dissolute, extravagant and unpopular, and had a string of mistresses.

While still Prince of Wales, his excessive eating and drinking had piled on the pounds. By 1797, he weighed 111 kilograms (245 pounds or 17½ stone), and by 1824 his waist measured 130 centimetres (50 inches). Morbidly obese, his appearance in public invited ridicule.

His exorbitant lifestyle also piled on another sort of pound. In 1795, his debts amounted to £630,000 (about £59,733,000 in today's money). He was rescued by Parliament, who granted him an extra £65,000 (approximately £6,163,000 today) per year, followed by a further £60,000 (£5,028,000) a few years later. His wasteful spending during the Napoleonic Wars also turned the public against him.

As for 'kissing the girls', he did plenty of this. Despite being married to Caroline of Brunswick (and an earlier illegal marriage to Maria Fitzherbert), he had numerous affairs with women, including an actress, a divorcée, and several married women from the aristocracy. Various illegitimate children were said to be the result.

Altogether, George's dissolute way of life and lack of respect for his royal role earned the contempt of his people – and perhaps inspired them to mock him in a nursery rhyme.

ROLY-POLY GEORGE?

Fourteen years after the death of George IV in 1830, the first printed version of the rhyme appeared in the 1844 edition of *The Nursery Rhymes of England*. It reads thus:

> Rowley Powley, pudding and pie,
> Kissed the girls and made them cry;
> When the girls begin to cry,
> Rowley Powley runs away.

'Rowley Powley' could be interpreted in the modern sense of 'roly-poly' – meaning 'with rolls of fat' – but the phrase, also spelt *rowle powle*, is an archaic term for a good-for-nothing fellow.

Humpty Dumpty Sat On a Wall

> Humpty Dumpty sat on a wall,
> Humpty Dumpty had a great fall.
> All the king's horses,
> And all the king's men,
> Couldn't put Humpty together again.

Illustrations to this very well-known rhyme usually show Humpty Dumpty as an egg. However, the words themselves do not say as much, perhaps because the rhyme was originally posed as a riddle: 'What object, if it fell down and broke, could not be repaired even by the most powerful forces in the land?'

Of unknown antiquity and obscure origins, it has invited various interpretations. Among them is the suggestion that Humpty was really King Richard III of England – popularly seen as a hunchback – who, despite the size of his army, was defeated at Bosworth Field in 1485. In the late seventeenth century 'humpty dumpty' was the name for a drink of brandy boiled with ale, while in the eighteenth century it was a slang term for a short and clumsy person. It is tempting (but probably wrong) to infer from this that Humpty was a squat, bumbling individual who fell off the wall when drunk.

Early printed versions of the rhyme appear in 1797 and 1803, while the 1846 edition of *The Nursery Rhymes of England* has this variation:

Humpty Dumpty lay in a beck.
With all his sinews round his neck;
Forty Doctors and forty wrights
Couldn't put Humpty Dumpty to rights!

CLOSE RELATIVES

'Humpty Dumpty' isn't the only name by which the character is known. Such is his appeal that he pops up all across Europe, in rhymes that have a similar content and form to the English version: in France he is Boule Boule; in Sweden, Thille Lille; in Finland, Hillerin-Lillerin; in Germany, Rüntzelten-Püntzelten. By 1906, he had even made it across the Atlantic Ocean to Pennsylvania, where his Pennsylvania Dutch name is Hobberti Bob.

Simple Simon Met a Pieman

Simple Simon met a pieman,
Going to the fair;
Says Simple Simon to the pieman,
Let me taste your ware.

Says the pieman to Simple Simon,
Show me first your penny;
Says Simple Simon to the pieman,
Indeed I have not any.

Simple Simon went a-fishing,
For to catch a whale;
All the water he had got
Was in his mother's pail.

Simple Simon went to look
If plums grew on a thistle;
He pricked his finger very much,
Which made poor Simon whistle.

He went for water with a sieve,
But soon it all ran through;
And now poor Simple Simon
Bids you all adieu.

Nursery rhymes do not bother with political correctness (the concept didn't exist when they originated) and this one mocks the mental abilities of someone who might now be dubbed 'developmentally challenged'. As a generic name for such a person, Simple Simon – a simpleton – goes back centuries. He has cropped up in chapbooks – small, illustrated, paper-covered booklets – since at least 1764, while a ballad entitled 'Simple Simon's Misfortunes and his Wife Margery's Cruelty' dates from 1685 or earlier.

CHAPTER 3

GRANDAMS AND GREYBEARDS

WHILE THE GREYBEARDS in this chapter are charmingly eccentric, it is the grandams who must be reckoned with. Far from being silly old biddies who do foolish things, old women, in their many guises, are central figures in folklore and myth, embodying the female power and wisdom that comes with age.

Grandams

Old Mother Goose

> Old Mother Goose,
> When she wanted to wander,
> Would ride through the air
> On a very fine gander.

This verse is the first of fifteen from a chapbook story, dating from the early nineteenth century, about a goose that laid golden eggs. In Britain and America, Mother Goose had become a familiar nursery rhyme character a century before, probably after John Newbery published *Mother Goose's Melody*, in about 1765.

In France, Mother Goose was associated with fairy tales, rather than nursery rhymes. These were sometimes known as *contes de ma Mère l'Oye* (tales of Mother Goose), a phrase that Charles Perrault used as a subtitle in his famous 1697 story collection *Histoires et contes du temps passé* (Stories and Tales of Times Past).

But this grandam is so much more than a nursery figure or pantomime dame; she is a key figure among the many crones who crowd the world of folk tale and myth. She derives her identity from the real-life disseminator of 'old wives' tales', from the lowly, aged children's nurse to the wise woman at the edge of the village; she is the spinner of yarns and the weaver of tales. Indeed, it is not hard to picture her regaling her audience as she sits at her wheel in the darkness of winter – after all, what else was there to do without television?

MOTHER GOOSE'S ALTER EGOS

Here are some of Mother Goose's close relations, who share the same gene pool:

1. The sinister crone who sits spinning at the top of the stairs in *Sleeping Beauty*, and Cinderella's

benign godmother, disguised as a ragged old woman.

2. Aphrodite, Greek goddess of love, who would ride through the air on the back of a goose, her sacred bird.

3. The French Queen Berthe, who was closely associated with storytelling and spinning, and was known as *La Reine Pédauque* (from *la reine pied d'oye*, or the goose-footed queen) because one of her feet was large, flat and goose-like.

4. *La Mère Cigogne* (Mother Stork), after another French name for fairy tales: *contes de la cigogne* (tales of the stork).

5. Gammer Grethel – 'gammer' being an archaic term for 'old wife' – a composite fictional figure based on the real Dorothea Viehmann, one of the main sources of the famous stories collected by the Brothers Grimm.

❧ ❀ ❧

Old Mother Hubbard

Old Mother Hubbard
Went to the cupboard,
To fetch her poor dog a bone;
But when she got there

The cupboard was bare
And so the poor dog had none.

She went to the baker's
To buy him some bread;
But when she came back
The poor dog was dead.

She went to the undertaker's
To buy him a coffin;
But when she came back
The poor dog was laughing.

She took a clean dish
To get him some tripe;
But when she came back
He was smoking a pipe.

She went to the alehouse
To get him some beer;
But when she came back
The dog sat in a chair.

She went to the tavern
For white wine and red;
But when she came back
The dog stood on his head.

She went to the fruiterer's
To buy him some fruit;
But when she came back
He was playing the flute.

She went to the tailor's
To buy him a coat;
But when she came back
He was riding a goat.

She went to the hatter's
To buy him a hat;
But when she came back
He was feeding the cat.

She went to the barber's
To buy him a wig;
But when she came back
He was dancing a jig.

She went to the cobbler's
To buy him some shoes;
But when she came back
He was reading the news.

She went to the seamstress
To buy him some linen;
But when she came back
The dog was a-spinning.

She went to the hosier's
To buy him some hose;
But when she came back
He was dressed in his clothes.

The dame made a curtsy,
The dog made a bow;
The dame said, Your servant,
The dog said, Bow-wow.

In 1804, so the story goes, Sarah Catherine Martin was staying with her future brother-in-law, John Pollexfen Bastard, in Devon. Irritated by Sarah's chattering, John told her to 'run away and write one of your stupid little rhymes'. The result was 'Old Mother Hubbard'. After publication in 1805 in book form under the title *The Comic Adventures of Old Mother Hubbard and Her Dog*, it became a bestseller, with 'upwards of ten thousand copies' distributed in a few months, and a reprint the following year.

Sarah Martin wrote that the original Mother Hubbard was a housekeeper in the Devon village where she had stayed, but 'Mother Hubbard', as a generic character, was known as early as the sixteenth century. There are several other 'Old Mothers' in nursery rhymes, too, such as Old Mother Shuttle and Old Mother Twitchett – as well as Old Dame Trot who had a cat rather than a dog. 'Old Dame Trot, and Her Comical Cat' was published in 1803, with verses that are remarkably similar to those of Mother Hubbard. However, the dame and her cat had been known for at least a hundred years prior to publication, so Sarah Martin may have been merely expanding on a rhyme already known in oral tradition.

✤ ❋ ✤

There Was an Old Woman

> There was an old woman
> Lived under a hill,
> And if she's not gone
> She lives there still.

Like 'I'll Tell You a Story (About Jack a Nory)' (see page 32), the first two lines of this rhyme set us up to expect that a story will follow. But all that we get is a statement of the obvious – 'if she's not gone, she lives there still'. End of story. This kind of humour appealed to the eighteenth-century mind, and a version of the rhyme first appeared in *The Academy of Complements* in 1714.

'There was an old woman' is a handy opening line because almost any story can be tacked onto it. Here are just some of the examples:

There was an old woman …

1. and nothing she had

2. had three cows, Rosy and Colin and Dun

3. had three sons, Jerry and James and John

4. sold puddings and pies

5. her name it was Peg

There Was an Old Woman Tossed Up in a Basket

> There was an old woman tossed up in a basket,
> Seventeen times as high as the moon;
> Where she was going I couldn't but ask it,
> For in her hand she carried a broom.
> Old woman, old woman, old woman, quoth I,
> Where are you going to up so high?
> To brush the cobwebs off the sky!
> May I go with you?
> Aye, by-and-by.

First recorded in *Mother Goose's Melody*, published in about 1765, this rhyme is usually sung to the tune of 'Lillibulero', a march that originated as an Irish jig that was known as long ago as the mid-seventeenth century.

Disregarding her gender, the 'old woman' has been variously associated with kings Henry V and James II. The original wording was probably 'tossed up in a blanket ninety-nine times as high as the moon', as in the ballad 'The Jacobite Tossed Up in a Blanket'. This may be where the connection with James II arose.

63

The followers of this Catholic Stuart king, who was deposed by his daughter Mary and her Protestant husband William, were known as Jacobites.

※ ✳ ※

There Was an Old Woman Who Lived in a Shoe

> There was an old woman who lived in a shoe,
> She had so many children she didn't know what
> to do;
> She gave them some broth without any bread;
> Then whipped them all soundly and put them
> to bed.

Several contenders have been put forward as the main character in this nursery rhyme, for no other reason than the size of their families. One is Queen Caroline, the wife of George II, who had eight children; another is Elizabeth Vergoose of Boston, who was renowned for the size of her family, having six children of her own and ten stepchildren, and who was also identified by some – on slender grounds – as being the original 'Mother Goose'.

The rhyme was first recorded in 1784 in *Gammer Gurton's Garland*, but a 1797 version, in a book entitled *Infant Institutes*, uses a Shakespearean word – 'a-loffeing' (for 'laughing') – which suggests that its origins may be considerably older. A 'beetle', or *betel*, is Old English for a beating implement, while 'to bespeak' means 'to order':

> There was a little old woman, and she liv'd in a shoe,
> She had so many children, she didn't know what
>   to do.
> She crumm'd 'em some porridge without any bread;
> And she borrow'd a beetle, and she knocked 'em
>   all o' the head.
> Then out went th' old woman to bespeak 'em a
>   coffin,
> And when she came back, she found 'em all a-
>   loffeing.

SHOE SYMBOLISM

The old woman's unlikely dwelling – a shoe – may be a metaphor. In folklore, shoes were significant symbols of female sexuality and fertility, and this 'old woman' was certainly fertile. In Anglo-Saxon England, the bride's shoe was passed from her father to her groom as a token of the latter's marriage rights, while the tradition of tying shoes to the newly-weds' car is a sort of good-luck wish that the union will be fruitful.

Greybeards

Old King Cole

Old King Cole
Was a merry old soul,
And a merry old soul was he;
He called for his pipe,
And he called for his bowl,
And he called for his fiddlers three.

Every fiddler, he had a fiddle,
And a very fine fiddle had he;
Twee tweedle dee, tweedle dee, went the fiddlers.
Oh, there's none so rare
As can compare
With King Cole and his fiddlers three.

The identity of named characters in nursery rhymes always invites speculation, and just who this jolly monarch might be was up for debate as far back as the early eighteenth century. In his *Useful Transactions in Philosophy* (1708–9), the satirist William King quoted the rhyme and favoured two possibilities: a medieval cloth merchant called Thomas Colebrook or, as he put it, 'the Prince that Built Colchester', on the supposition that the city was named after this royal personage. William Chappell, the nineteenth-century authority on popular music, supported

King's first theory, stating that Colebrook was commonly known as 'Old Cole'.

First rendered as the lyrics to a song, 'Old King Cole' was popular throughout the eighteenth century. It was particularly so in Scotland, perhaps because of the assertion by the famous Scottish author Sir Walter Scott that 'Auld King Coul' was the father of the mythical Celtic warrior hero Finn Mac Cumhal (pronounced Mac Cool), also known as Fingal.

❧ ✳ ❧

One Misty, Moisty Morning

> One misty, moisty, morning,
> When cloudy was the weather,
> There I met an old man
> Clothed all in leather;
> Clothed all in leather,
> With cap under his chin.
> How do you do, and how do you do,
> And how do you do again?

This made it into the nursery, at least in printed form, in the early nineteenth century. But in fact it's a lot older, being the first of fifteen verses of an old ballad printed in about 1680. Entitled 'The Wiltshire Wedding' it tells the story of the wedding between

'Daniel Do-well and Doll the Dairy-Maid. With the Consent of old Father Leather-Coat, and her dear and tender Mother Plodwell'. The seventeenth-century wording runs:

All in a misty Morning,
So cloudy was the Weather,
I meeting with an old Man,
Who was cloathed all in Leather,
With ne'er a Shirt unto his Back,
But Woollen to his Skin.
With how do you do, and how do you do,
And how do you do again.

There Was a Crooked Man

There was a crooked man, and he walked a
    crooked mile;
He found a crooked sixpence against a crooked stile;
He bought a crooked cat, which caught a crooked
    mouse,
And they all lived together in a little crooked house.

'There was a [crooked/little/old/mad] man' is the nursery rhyme equivalent of 'Once upon a time' – it's a good story opener and sets the scene for the forthcoming narrative, for example:

- There was a little man, and he had a little gun …
- There was a little man, and he woo'ed a little maid …
- There was a mad man and he had a mad wife …
- There was a man who had no eyes …
- There was an old man in a velvet coat …

The 'crooked man' was first recorded in 1842 in *The Nursery Rhymes of England*. One literal interpretation suggests that the rhyme was inspired by the crooked half-timbered houses in Lavenham, Suffolk, that lean against each other at irregular angles. Another interprets it metaphorically as a political jibe: the 'crooked man' was the wily Scottish general Sir Alexander Leslie, who successfully led the Covenanters – a Scottish Presbyterian movement – in the Bishops' Wars (1639–40) against Charles I, after the king tried to impose religious control on Scotland, while the 'crooked stile' and the 'crooked house' were, respectively, the uneasy border between Scotland and England and the wary truce that they shared.

CHAPTER 4

CHILDREN AT PLAY AND ASLEEP

BEHIND THE WORDS, nursery rhymes often open a window onto social history and folk belief. That is especially true of the rhymes here, which take us on a journey into the age-old world of children and the adults who cared for and guided them from cradle to school.

Playtime

Boys and Girls Come Out to Play

Boys and girls come out to play,
The moon doth shine as bright as day.
Leave your supper and leave your sleep,
And join your playfellows in the street.
Come with a whoop and come with a call,
Come with a good will or not at all.

Up the ladder and down the wall,
A half-penny loaf will serve us all;
You find milk, and I'll find flour,
And we'll have a pudding in half an hour.

The earliest references to this children's song appear in dance books for adults, in a political broadside and in satires that were published between 1708 and 1728. Even then, however, the verse appears to have been more strongly associated with the nursery than the adult world, and may date back to the middle of the previous century.

The first six lines were recorded in *Tommy Thumb's Pretty Song Book* in 1744, while the 1765 edition of *Mother Goose's Melody* includes an illustration of children playing by moonlight, captioned 'Boys and Girls come out to play'. The call to nocturnal play may allude to the fact that children once had to work during the day and were only free to play after the sun had gone down, when they might dance in a circle or skip to the words.

❦ ❈ ❦

Here We Go Round the Mulberry Bush

Here we go round the mulberry bush,
The mulberry bush, the mulberry bush,
Here we go round the mulberry bush,
On a cold and frosty morning.

This is the way we wash our face,
Wash our face,
Wash our face.
This is the way we wash our face
On a cold and frosty morning.

This is the way we comb our hair,
Comb our hair,
Comb our hair.
This is the way we comb our hair
On a cold and frosty morning.

This is the way we brush our teeth,
Brush our teeth,
Brush our teeth.
This is the way we brush our teeth
On a cold and frosty morning.

This is the way we put on our clothes,
Put on our clothes,
Put on our clothes.
This is the way we put on our clothes
On a cold and frosty morning.

This children's song and accompanying game was first recorded in *Popular Rhymes and Nursery Tales* in 1849. One interpretation of the words is that they parody England's futile attempts in the eighteenth and nineteenth centuries to rival China in silk production. Silkworms are reared on mulberry trees but the English planted the wrong kind of mulberries. This theory can apply only to the first four lines, of course. The subsequent lines are clearly action rhymes: children hold hands and move round in a circle to the first verse, then separate to imitate the actions described in each of the following verses.

Another, and possibly older, version cites a bramble bush, while a Scandinavian parallel has a juniper bush.

Here We Go Gathering Nuts in May

Here we go gathering nuts in May,
Nuts in May, nuts in May,
Here we go gathering nuts in May,
On a cold and frosty morning.

Who will you have for nuts in May,
Nuts in May, nuts in May,
Who will you have for nuts in May,
On a cold and frosty morning?

We'll have [name] for nuts in May,
Nuts in May, nuts in May,
We'll have [name] for nuts in May,
On a cold and frosty morning.

Who will you send to fetch [him/her] away,
Fetch [him/her] away, fetch [him/her] away,
Who will you send to fetch [him/her] away,
On a cold and frosty morning?

We'll send [name] to fetch [him/her] away,
Fetch [him/her] away, fetch [him/her] away,
We'll send [name] to fetch [him/her] away,
On a cold and frosty morning.

Set to the same tune as the previous rhyme, this is another singing game for children. It first appeared in print in *The Traditional Games of England, Scotland and Ireland*, in around 1894. In verses three and five, in answer to verses two and four, the children insert the name of one of their group and amend the pronoun (him/her) to the correct gender.

As to the nuts they are supposedly gathering, this would not be possible: nuts would not have formed, let alone ripened, in May, which is late spring in Northern Europe. 'Nuts in May' could be a corruption of 'knots of may', 'may' being another name for hawthorn, which would be blossoming then. Another possibility are the edible tubers of a wild flower known as the pignut, which can be harvested after the plant has flowered.

Ring-a-ring o' Roses

Ring-a-ring o' roses,
A pocket full of posies,
A-tishoo! A-tishoo!
We all fall down.

The cows are in the meadow
Lying fast asleep,
A-tishoo! A-tishoo!
We all get up again.

The first verse of this popular rhyme has become the standardized modern form of earlier printed variants, while the second verse derives from oral tradition.

The rhyme accompanies a children's ring dance: holding hands, the children dance around in a circle while singing the song; when they get to the last line – 'We all fall down' – they tumble to the floor or ground. The second verse allows them to jump up again. Another way to play the game is to dance around a child in the middle; whoever is last to 'fall down' then takes that child's place. In some versions, as in one regional variant from Yorkshire and another from late eighteenth-century Massachusetts, children did not fall down but squatted, curtsied or bowed at the fourth line.

UNIVERSAL RHYME

Surprisingly for such a well-known rhyme, 'Ring-a-ring o' Roses' does not appear in print before 1881, in Britain at least. But in 1790s Massachusetts, children were said to chant the following (without the famous 'A-tishoo'):

> Ring a ring a rosie
> A bottle full of posie,
> All the girls in our town,
> Ring for little Josie …

'Ring-a-ring o' Roses' is one of those travelling rhymes that seeds itself anywhere and everywhere, although we may not know the original soil in which it grew. Working in the late nineteenth-century, the folklorist Alice Gomme found twelve different versions, while *Shropshire Folk-Lore*, published in 1883, includes:

> A ring, a ring o' roses,
> A pocket-full o' posies;
> One for Jack, and one for Jim,
> And one for little Moses.
> A-tisha! a-tisha! a-tisha!

German children enjoy the following:

Ringel, Ringel, Reihe,
Wir sind der Kinder dreie,
Wir sitzen unter'm Holderbusch
Und machen alle husch, husch, husch!

Loosely translated, this reads: 'Ring, ring, row / We are children three / We're sitting under the elder bush / And all of us going, hush, hush, hush.'

There are closely related singing rhymes for Swiss, French, Italian, Irish, Dutch and Slavic children – and even this for little Gaelic-speakers:

Bulla! Bulla! Baisín,
Ta'n bo sa gùirdín.
Síos libh! Síos libh!
Éirigidh anois, Éirigidh!
Déanam arís é.

A rough translation reads: 'Clap! Clap! Hands, / The cow is in the garden. / Down you go! Down you go! / Get up now, get up! / Let's do it again.'

WHAT DOES IT MEAN?

All kinds of hidden meanings have been attributed to this singing game:

1. It's pagan in origin, based on the old belief that gifted children had the ability to laugh roses

out of their mouths, as cited by Jacob Grimm in *Deutsche Mythologie* (*Teutonic Mythology*).

2. The first line derives from *rosier*, the French word for rosebush, and the 'rosie' is the child standing in the centre of the circle of dancers.

3. It refers to the Great Plague that devastated London's population in 1665: the 'roses' describe the rash that was a symptom of the disease; the 'posies' were the bunches of herbs people carried as protection; 'a-tishoo' was the sneezing that accompanied the illness; and 'all fall down' was the inevitable death that followed. This interpretation has gained a foothold in the popular imagination – but there is one problem: it isn't true. Folklorists have discredited this theory, which did not make an appearance until the twentieth century. The wording on which it is based appears only in later versions of the rhyme; the alleged symptoms do not match those of plague especially well; and in many versions of the game children just bowed or curtsied rather than literally fell down.

Good Children, Naughty Children

There Was a Little Girl Who Had a Little Curl

> There was a little girl who had a little curl,
> Right in the middle of her forehead;
> And when she was good, she was very, very good,
> But when she was bad, she was horrid.

Although generally attributed to the American poet Henry Wadsworth Longfellow (1807–82), there is still some doubt as to the accuracy of this claim because the choice of words does not accord with the poet's usual style. It has also been credited to Thomas Bailey Aldrich (1836–1907), another American poet and writer. But neither may be the author: in 1946, an academic discussion in the *Papers of the Bibliographical Society of America* stated that the verse was first recorded in an anonymous broadside – a sort of poster or flyer – dating from before 1870. Whatever its origins, the rhyme has established a strong footing in the United States.

There are two further verses detailing some 'horrid' behaviour:

One day she went upstairs, while her parents, unawares,
In the kitchen down below were occupied with meals;
And she stood upon her head, on her little truckle bed,
And she then began hooraying with her heels.

Her mother heard the noise, and thought it was the boys
A-playing at a combat in the attic;
But when she climbed the stair, and found Jemima there,
She took and she did whip her most emphatic.

<hr/>

What Are Little Boys Made Of?

What are little boys made of?
What are little boys made of?
    Frogs and snails
    And puppy-dogs' tails,
That's what little boys are made of.

What are little girls made of?
What are little girls made of?
    Sugar and spice
    And all things nice,
That's what little girls are made of.

Such gender stereotypes may jar in contemporary ears, but this rhyme dates back to the nineteenth century, when social norms were different. It has been attributed to the English poet Robert Southey (1774–1843) but is not found in any of his printed works. The first-known recording was in the 1844 edition of *The Nursery Rhymes of England*.

Several nineteenth- and early twentieth-century nursery-rhyme and folklore collectors quoted the following lines:

- What are young men made of? Sighs and leers and crocodile tears.
- What are young women made of? Ribbons and laces, and sweet pretty faces.
- What are old women made of? Bushes and thorns and old cow's horns.
- What are our sailors made of, made of? Pitch and tar, pig-tail and scar.
- What are our soldiers made of, made of? Pipeclay and drill, the foeman to kill.

Sleeping Babies

Bye, Baby Bunting

Bye, baby bunting,
Daddy's gone a-hunting,
Gone to get a rabbit skin
To wrap the baby bunting in.

Gammer Gurton's Garland first recorded this lullaby in 1784. 'Bunting' is an old term of endearment, probably meaning 'plump'. In alternative verses, the baby is promised other forms of swaddling – a hare's skin, a calf's skin, a lion's skin, or a lamb's skin, as in the Scottish rhyme:

Hushie ba, burdie beeton,
Your Mammie's gane to Seaton,
For to buy a lammie's skin
To wrap your bonnie boukie in.

A verse from 1805 varies the wording and number of lines:

Bye, baby bunting,
Father's gone a hunting,
Mother's gone a milking
Sister's gone a silking,
Brother's gone to buy a skin
To wrap the baby bunting in.

In Orkney, off the coast of Scotland, the baby's mother heads off to buy 'a bullie's skin, tae rock wir bonnie bairnie in', probably so that she can rock her infant in the traditional way in a hammock of 'bullie' or calfskin.

❧ ❅ ❧

Rock-a-bye Baby, On the Tree Top

> Rock-a-bye baby, on the tree top,
> When the wind blows the cradle will rock;
> When the bough breaks, the cradle will fall,
> Down will come baby, cradle and all.

What dark-hearted crooner would want to threaten an innocent babe with these ominous words? Nevertheless, 'Rock-a-bye Baby' is one of the most widespread lullabies in the English-speaking world, traditionally sung to a variant of the old Irish jig 'Lillibulero' (as used for 'There Was an Old Woman Tossed Up in a Basket', page 63). Neither the age of the rhyme nor the tune can definitely be ascertained, but the printed verse is first found in *Mother Goose's Melody* in around 1765.

WHAT DOES IT MEAN?

Here are some of the theories as to the lullaby's origins and meaning:

- It is intended to 'serve as a Warning to the Proud and Ambitious, who climb so high that they generally fall at last', according to a footnote in *Mother Goose's Melody*.
- It refers to Horus the Child, the infant form of the Egyptian sun god, the adult Horus, according to Gerald Massey, the nineteenth-century writer on spiritualism and Egyptology.
- It was penned by a youth travelling with the Pilgrim Fathers on the *Mayflower* after he witnessed the way that Native American mothers rocked their babies in birch-bark cradles suspended from the branches of trees.
- It is a lampoon of the British royal line in the era of the Stuart king, James II (1603–1701), a time of rumours of illegitimate heirs, strife between Catholics and Protestants, and the final fall of the royal House of Stuart.

One obvious explanation is missing here: it seems likely that women once did rock their babies by suspending them in cradles or hammocks so that the wind could do the work – just like the mother in the Orkney version of 'Bye, Baby Bunting', above.

Bedtime Habits

Early to Bed and Early to Rise

Early to bed and early to rise
Makes a man healthy, wealthy and wise.

This morally improving proverb has been addressed to children for centuries. Perhaps Sir Anthony Fitzherbert (1470–1538) attributed his success as a judge, scholar and writer to a similar saying, for he recalled: 'At gramer scole I lerned a verse & that is this: *Sanat, santificat et ditat surgere mane.* That is to say, erly rysynge maketh a man hole in body, holer in soule, & richer in goodes.'

Hugh Rhodes, author of *The Boke of Nurture for Men, Seruauntes and Chyldren,* published in 1545, endorsed Sir Anthony's sentiments:

Ryse you earely in the morning, for it hath
    proper-tyes three:
Holynesse, health, and happy welth, as my Father
    taught mee.

The rhyme as we know it first appeared in 1639, in John Clarke's collection of proverbs for schoolchildren, *Paroemiologia Anglo-Latina.* There are versions in French and German too. In America, Benjamin Franklin – scientist, inventor and a founding father of the United States – popularized the saying in the 1735 edition of his *Poor Richard's Almanack*, an annual journal that he published under the pseudonym Poor Richard.

❧ ✳ ❧

Matthew, Mark, Luke and John

> Matthew, Mark, Luke and John,
> Bless the bed that I lie on.
> Four corners to my bed,
> Four angels round my head;
> One to watch and one to pray
> And two to bear my soul away.

This innocuous little rhyme seems at first to be as innocent and transparent as the little children who traditionally recited it at bedtime, invoking the protection of the saints to whom the four Gospels of the Bible's New Testament are attributed. Often known as a type of 'Paternoster' or prayer (from *Pater Noster*, 'Our Father', the first two words in the Latin version of the Lord's Prayer), it was indeed almost the only prayer children once knew.

Some versions run to four verses, as in this 1891 variant collected by the Anglican priest, scholar and writer Sabine Baring-Gould, beginning:

> Matthew, Mark, Luke and John,
> Bless this bed that I lie on;
> Four angels to my bed,

Two to bottom, two to head,
Two to hear me when I pray,
Two to bear my soul away.

THE DARK SIDE

In 1665, the English physician Thomas Ady published *A Candle in the Dark: Or, A Treatise Concerning the Nature of Witches and Witchcraft*. In this sceptical study of what was then branded 'witchcraft', he showed his disapproval both of superstition and of the Catholic Church (which seemed to him to be much the same thing) when he recounted: 'An old Woman in Essex who was living in my time, she had lived also in Queen Maries [Mary Tudor's] time, had learned thence many Popish Charms, one whereof was this; every night when she lay down to sleep she charmed her Bed, saying:

Matthew, Mark, Luke and John,
The Bed be blest that I lye on.'

After repeating this spell three times, Ady continues, the old woman then felt it safe to go to sleep.

Scottish Presbyterian George Sinclair revealed a darker practice in *Satan's Invisible World Discovered*, published in 1685. He tells of a 'witch' who recited a similar 'Black' Paternoster, a night-time charm, to ward off evil:

Four newks [corners] in this house, for haly
    [holy] Angels,
A post in the midst, that's Christ Jesus,
Lucas, Marcus, Matthew, Joannes,
God be into this house, and all that belangs
    [belongs to] us.

THE FOUR CORNERS

Any verse that resonates so strongly in folk
conscience must have deep roots and be widely
disseminated. As far back as 1387, Geoffrey Chaucer
cited a Paternoster in 'The Miller's Tale', one of the
stories in his *Canterbury Tales*, which recalls the
rhyme here. And in late fifteenth-century Germany
children said a similar bedtime prayer, which called
on *zwölf engel* – twelve angels – to accompany them
into sleep: two at their head, two at their sides,
two at their feet, two to guard them, two to wake
them, two to lead them to the *himlischen paradeise* –
heavenly paradise. There are related rhymes in many
other European countries and languages, including
France, Spain and Denmark.

Clearly the idea of spiritual beings protecting us
in that most vulnerable of states – sleep – touches
something very profound. There is also a noticeable
pattern in all variants of the rhyme: the angels are
often grouped in pairs; and they are placed in four

stations, at the head, foot and either side of the sleeper, or effectively north, south, east and west. With angelic sentries posted at the four corners of the bed – or corners of the world – the sleeper is fully protected.

This image draws from a deep reservoir of ages-old magical thinking. An esoteric Jewish prayer designed to be recited before sleep invokes the protection of four guardian angels: 'At my right Michael, at my left Gabriel, before me Uriel, behind me Raphael ...' Even further back in time, the ancient Babylonians intoned: 'Shamash before me, behind me Sin, Nergal at my right, Ninib at my left ...'

A HUMBLE REQUEST

This children's bedtime prayer bypasses saints and angels and petitions God directly. It was widely disseminated during the eighteenth century and was especially popular in the United States:

> Now I lay me down to sleep,
> I pray the Lord my soul to keep;
> If I should die before I wake,
> I pray the Lord my soul to take.

Wee Willie Winkie Runs Through the Town

Wee Willie Winkie runs through the town,
Up stairs and down stairs in his night-gown,
Tapping at the window, crying at the lock,
Are the children in their bed, for it's past ten
o'clock?

This familiar rhyme is the best-known work to come from the pen of Glaswegian woodturner and cabinet-maker William Miller. His poems appeared in various magazines, but in 1842 'Willie Winkie' and others were published as a collection under the title *Whistle-binkie; Stories for the Fireside*.

This is the better-known English version, for Miller's original was written in the Scots language:

Wee Willie Winkie rins through the toon,
Up stairs an' doon stairs in his nicht-gown,
Tirling [twiddling] at the window, crying at the
lock,
Are the weans [young children] in their bed, for
it's now ten o'clock?

Altogether there are five verses, only the first has passed into popular circulation. The second of the five verses, in English and Scots respectively, runs:

Hey, Willie Winkie, are you coming in?
The cat is singing purring sounds to the sleeping
hen,

The dog's spread out on the floor, and doesn't give
    a cheep,
But here's a wakeful little boy who will not fall
    asleep!

Hey, Willie Winkie, are ye coming ben?
The cat's singing grey thrums to the sleeping hen,
The dog's spelder'd on the floor, and disna gi'e a
    cheep,
But here's a waukrife laddie! that winna fa' asleep.

'Willie Winkie' was a nickname that the opposing
Jacobites used for the Protestant William III, who
took the throne of England, Scotland and Ireland
in 1689. However, it is unlikely that the Willie
referred to here is this monarch, since he had been
dead some 140 years by the time the rhyme was
written.

A highly popular fictional figure, Willie Winkie
joins the ranks of other sleep- and dream-bringers,
along with the Celtic Dream Angus, Hans Christian
Andersen's Ole Lukøje and the Sandman of
European folklore.

CHAPTER 5

ALL HUMAN LIFE

NURSERY RHYMES REFLECT everyday life, but it's not the twenty-first-century life we know, of office workers and IT specialists and financial traders; it's a vanished world of shepherds and bakers and cobblers and candlestick makers and – tucked within the folds of the rhymes – the odd woman of easy virtue.

Country Folk

Baa, Baa, Black Sheep

> Baa, baa, black sheep,
> Have you any wool?
> Yes, sir, yes, sir,
> Three bags full;
> One for the master,
> And one for the dame,
> And one for the little boy
> Who lives down the lane.

First published in 1744 in *Tommy Thumb's Pretty Song Book* – the oldest anthology of English nursery rhymes – the wording of this rhyme has hardly changed in more than two centuries.

There is a theory that it refers to resentment at the heavy taxation imposed on wool in England during the Middle Ages. The version ending 'none for the little boy that cries down the lane' does have more of a political undertone, with the little boy perhaps representing the peasantry and the master and dame the ruling class. Another, more recent, interpretation is that the rhyme alludes to the Slave Trade, particularly in the Deep South of the United States.

'Baa, Baa, Black Sheep' is sung to a tune similar to that used for 'Twinkle, Twinkle, Little Star' (see page 151).

Little Bo-Peep Has Lost Her Sheep

Little Bo-Peep has lost her sheep,
And doesn't know where to find them;
Leave them alone, and they'll come home,
Bringing their tails behind them.

Little Bo-Peep fell fast asleep,
And dreamt she heard them bleating;
But when she awoke, she found it a joke,
For they were still a-fleeting.

Then up she took her little crook,
Determined for to find them;
She found them indeed, but it made her heart bleed,
For they'd left their tails behind them.

It happened one day, as Bo-Peep did stray
Into a meadow hard by,
There she espied their tails side by side,
All hung on a tree to dry.

She heaved a sigh and wiped her eye,
And over the hillocks went rambling,
And tried what she could, as a shepherdess should,
To tack each again to its lambkin.

One of the most famous of all English nursery
rhymes, this surprisingly was not recorded until
1805, by the English antiquarian Francis Douce –
and that was only the first verse. Attempts to give a
long history to the rhyme and to attribute meaning
to it have not met with success. However, as a babies'
or children's game similar to
peek-a-boo, 'bo-peep' goes
back a long way:

1. The earliest reference to the game seems to be in 1364. As punishment for giving a short measure of ale, a woman called Alice Causton had to 'play bo-pepe thorowe a pillery'; in other words, she was placed in a pillory, with her head and hands 'playing peek-a-boo' through the holes.

2. In Shakespeare's time playful sheep were everywhere, as in this Elizabethan ballad:

   > Halfe England ys nowght now but shepe,
   > In everye corner they play boe-pepe.

3. Nineteenth-century children played bo-peep while reciting the following rhyme:

   > Bo-Peep, Little Bo-Peep,
   > Now's the time for hide and seek.

Little Boy Blue, Come Blow Your Horn

Little Boy Blue,
Come blow your horn,
The sheep's in the meadow,
The cow's in the corn.
But where is the boy
Who looks after the sheep?
He's under a haystack,
Fast asleep.

Will you wake him?
No, not I,
For if I do,
He's sure to cry.

According to one theory, 'Little Boy Blue' was really Cardinal Thomas Wolsey, Lord Chancellor to Henry VIII. Wolsey was the son of an Ipswich butcher and, as a boy, would certainly have looked after his father's livestock. However, no convincing evidence has been found to support this idea.

The earliest printed version of the rhyme is in *The Famous Tommy Thumb's Little Story-book*, from around 1760. A similar verse appears in Shakespeare's *King Lear*, written in about 1603, when Edgar, masquerading as Mad Tom, says:

Sleepest or wakest thou, jolly shepheard?
Thy sheepe be in the corne;
And for one blast of thy minikin mouth
Thy sheepe shall take no harme.

This suggests that the rhyme – or rather its content – dates back to well before its first printing; but the idea of a sleeping shepherd is not exactly hard to conjure in the mind's eye and may be more of a generic theme.

This Is the Way the Ladies Ride

> This is the way the ladies ride:
> Nimmy-nim-nim, nimmy-nim-nim,
> This is the way the ladies ride:
> Nimmy-nim-nimmy, nim-nim,
>
> This is the way the gentlemen ride:
> Gallop-a-trot, gallop-a-trot!
> This is the way the gentlemen ride:
> Gallop-a-gallop-a-trot!
>
> This is the way the farmers ride:
> Hobbledy-hoy, hobbledy-hoy!
> This is the way the farmers ride:
> Hobbledy hobbledy-hoy!

Despite grating on modern ears, the cultural stereotypes in this rhyme probably washed over the heads of previous generations, who were happy just to get on with singing the song and playing the game: a child, seated on an adult's knee, is bounced up and down or rolled about to the second and fourth lines of each verse. The fun is in the anticipation.

First appearing, in a slightly different form, in the 1842 edition of *The Nursery Rhymes of England*, the rhyme appealed to all nationalities. There are thirteen Scottish versions, for example, as well as German, French and American variants.

To Market, to Market, to Buy a Fat Pig

To market, to market, to buy a fat pig,
Home again, home again, jiggety-jig.
To market, to market, to buy a fat hog,
Home again, home again, jiggety-jog.

Another knee-bouncing game like the previous rhyme, this is the present-day wording, but the earliest printed version dates back to 1805, in *Songs for the Nursery*, and goes thus:

To market, to market, to buy a penny bun,
Home again, home again, market is done.

A 'plum bun' was later substituted for a 'penny bun'. The 'jiggety-jig/jog' of the modern rhyme allows a child to be placed on an adult's knee and bobbed up and down to the words.

Tradespeople

Cobbler, Cobbler, Mend My Shoe

Cobbler, cobbler, mend my shoe.
Get it done by half past two.
Half past two is much too late!
Get it done by half past eight.

Stitch it up, and stitch it down,
And I'll give you half a crown.

Although there is an earlier form of the rhyme, this wording did not appear, in print at least, until the early to mid-twentieth century. The verse can be used in the children's game 'Hunt the Slipper' which is similar to 'Pass the Parcel' and was an especially popular parlour game in the eighteenth century. Children sit in a circle, playing the part of cobblers; another child, playing the part of a customer, hands an old slipper or shoe to one of the 'cobblers' while reciting the rhyme and closing his or her eyes. As the 'customer' counts to ten or leaves the room, the 'cobblers' secretly pass the slipper around the circle; the customer then joins in again and has to guess which cobbler has the shoe.

Rub-a-dub-dub

Rub-a-dub-dub,
Three men in a tub,
And who do you think they be?
The butcher, the baker, the candlestick maker,
They all jumped out of a rotten potato,
'Twas enough to make a man stare.

As with so many nursery rhymes, at first we take it at face value ... but the words don't really make sense

– just why are three grown men sitting in a tub? The
earliest recordings of the verse throw a different light
on the matter:

> Hey! rub-a-dub-dub, ho! rub-a-dub, three maids
>   in a tub,
> And who do you think were there?
> The butcher, the baker, the candlestick maker,
> And all of them gone to the fair.

The butcher, the baker and the candlestick maker
have been caught in the act! These apparently
respectable members of the community have been
spied at a local fair watching a kind of peep-show
and ogling the three young women on display there.

❧ ✳ ❧

See-saw, Margery Daw

> See-saw Margery Daw,
> Jacky shall have a new master;
> Jacky shall earn but a penny a day,
> Because he can't work any faster.

The generic name Jacky is sometimes replaced with
the equally generic Johnny or Tommy. There is
social commentary in this rhyme – first printed in
Mother Goose's Melody in about 1765 – and in this
lesser-known variant:

See-saw, Margery Daw,
Sold her bed and lay upon straw;
Sold her bed and lay upon hay,
And pisky came and carried her away.
For wasn't she a dirty slut
To sell her bed and lie in the dirt?

The first and better-known version is traditionally sung by children as they play on the see-saw. But there is no written record of the game much before 1700, and the phrase 'see-saw' goes back further. In his play *The Antipodes*, printed in 1640, Richard Brome uses the word and associates it with sawyers, men who saw timber for a living: 'you brought me to towne wi' yee, With see saw sacke a downe, like a Sawyer'. It's possible that the rhyme was originally a work song for sawyers to help them move rhythmically back and forth when using a two-handled saw. This theory also helps to explain the last two lines.

As for 'Margery Daw', 'daw' is archaic English for 'sluggard' – a lazy person; in Scotland it indicates an 'untidy woman, a slattern'. And in the eighteenth and nineteenth centuries, Margery was a name used almost exclusively by the rural poor. All of this tells us that both versions of the rhyme are referring to the world of the less privileged classes of society.

Ways of the World

Come Let's to Bed

> Come let's to bed,
> Says Sleepy-head;
> Tarry a while, says Slow;
> Put on the pan,
> Says Greedy Nan,
> Let's sup before we go.

Small variations have been made to this rhyme without changing the general sense. The first printed version, in *Gammer Gurton's Garland* of 1784, quotes: 'Sit up a while, says Slow; / Hang on the pot ...' The important thing is to maintain the rhyme, so if 'pot' replaces 'pan', 'Greedy Gut' can then replace 'Greedy Nan'. Greedy Nan has also occasionally transitioned into Greedy Dan, and Greedy Gut into Greedy Sot. In 1872, *Notes and Queries*, a long-running scholarly journal, gave another alternative:

> To bed, to bed, says Drowsy-head;
> Not so fast, says Slow;
> Put on the pot, says Greedy Gut,
> We'll sup before we go.

Not much else can be said about this rhyme other than that the characters reveal their very human natures: each insists on a different response according to his or her personal preference, priorities and characteristics.

Elsie Marley is Grown So Fine

Elsie Marley is grown so fine,
She won't get up to feed the swine,
But lies in bed till eight or nine.
Lazy Elsie Marley.

A rarity in nursery rhymes with their imagined characters, the Elsie Marley here was a real person. The verse is the first of a song about her dating from the mid-eighteenth century and printed in about 1756. Another version of the song, collected in 1784, identifies her as Alice Marley, the celebrated 'alewife' or landlady of The Swan pub in Picktree, near Chester-le-Street in the northeast of England. Married to Ralph Marley, she was, by contemporary accounts, tall, slender, attractive, bubbling with personality and not short of male admirers – indeed, she had a certain reputation that had nothing to do with the way she served ale.

But despite her fame and popularity, she came to a sad end. On 5 August 1768, a local record noted the death of 'the well-known Alice Marley' who, suffering from a fever, 'got out of her house and went into a field where there was an old coal-pit full of water, which she fell into and was drowned'. She was buried two days later, on 7 August.

✻

Hark, Hark, the Dogs Do Bark

> Hark, hark, the dogs do bark,
> The beggars are coming to town.
> Some in rags and some in jags,
> And one in a velvet gown.

Gammer Gurton's Garland of 1784 was the first to print this rhyme, with minor variations in the wording. There has been much speculation as to its meaning and age, including:

- It recalls the conditions in Tudor England when wandering beggars were so numerous that they were becoming a menace. More specifically, some say, it refers to the Dissolution of the Monasteries in the 1530s, when Henry VIII disbanded the Roman Catholic monasteries and dispossessed the monks living in them, and their dependants, creating a throng of homeless itinerants.

- It dates to the Tudor period because 'jag' was the name for the popular Tudor fashion of making a slit in parts of a garment, such as the sleeves, to reveal the fabric underneath, as can be seen in portraits of Henry VIII.
- It refers to the Dutch followers of William III, who took the English throne during the Glorious Revolution of 1688–9. 'Beggars' is thought to have been common slang for the Dutch, and the 'one in a velvet gown' may have been the new king himself.

※ ❋ ※

Hickety, Pickety, My Black Hen

> Hickety, pickety, my black hen,
> She lays eggs for gentlemen;
> Gentlemen come every day
> To see what my black hen doth lay.
> Sometimes nine and sometimes ten,
> Hickety, pickety, my black hen.

This rhyme did not make its first appearance in print until the mid-nineteenth century, in the 1853 edition of *The Nursery Rhymes of England*. 'Hen' was affectionate seventeenth- and eighteenth-century slang for 'woman' – a term still used in some parts of Britain – and on closer examination the wording

does have suggestive connotations. The verse may be a newer variant of the more explicit 'Little Blue Betty', who first showed up on the printed page in *Gammer Gurton's Garland* in the 1810 edition, and was apparently based on a real-life 'woman of easy virtue' who worked in a public house called *The Golden Can*:

Little Blue Betty lived in a den,
She sold good ale to gentlemen;
Gentlemen came every day,
And little Blue Betty hopped away,
She hopped upstairs to make her bed,
And she tumbled down and broke her head.

CHAPTER 6

WOOINGS AND WEDDINGS

NOT ALL IS hearts and flowers in the rhymes that follow. There are smitten sweethearts, for sure, but feisty country girls are not fooled by smooth words, while one overburdened husband is forced to hide his wife away in a pumpkin shell.

Wooings

A Frog He Would a-Wooing Go

A frog he would a-wooing go,
Heigh ho! says Rowley,
A frog he would a-wooing go,
Whether his mother would let him or no.
With a rowley, powley, gammon, and spinach,
Heigh ho! says Anthony Rowley.

So off he set with his opera hat,
Heigh ho! says Rowley,
So off he set with his opera hat,
And on the road he met with a rat,
With a rowley, powley [etc].

Pray, Mister Rat, will you go with me?
Heigh ho! says Rowley,
Pray, Mister Rat will you go with me,
Kind Mrs Mousey for to see?
With a rowley, powley [etc].

They came to the door of Mousey's hall,
Heigh ho! says Rowley,
They gave a loud knock, and they gave a loud call.
With a rowley, powley [etc].

Pray, Mrs Mouse are you within?
Heigh ho! says Rowley,
Oh yes, kind sirs, I'm sitting to spin.
With a rowley, powley [etc].

Pray, Mrs Mouse will you give us some beer?
Heigh ho! says Rowley,
For Froggy and I are fond of good cheer.
With a rowley, powley [etc].

Pray, Mr Frog will you give us a song?
Heigh ho! says Rowley,
Let it be something that's not very long.
With a rowley, powley [etc].

Indeed, Mrs Mouse, replied Mr Frog,
Heigh ho! says Rowley,
A cold has made me as hoarse as a dog.
With a rowley, powley [etc].

Since you have a cold, Mr Frog, Mousey said,
Heigh ho! says Rowley,
I'll sing you a song that I've just made.
With a rowley, powley [etc].

But while they were all a-merry-making,
Heigh ho! says Rowley,
A cat and her kittens came tumbling in.
With a rowley, powley [etc].

The cat she seized the rat by the crown,
Heigh ho! says Rowley,
The kittens they pulled the little mouse down.
With a rowley, powley [etc].

This put Mr Frog in a terrible fright,
Heigh ho! says Rowley.
He took up his hat and he wished them good-
night.
With a rowley, powley [etc].

But as Froggy was crossing over a brook,
Heigh ho! says Rowley,
A lily-white duck came and gobbled him up.
With a rowley, powley [etc].

So there was the end of one, two, three,
Heigh ho! says Rowley,
The rat, the mouse, and the little frogg-ee.
With a rowley, powley [etc].

The verses above are the best known and most recent of a long narrative song with a history going back more than four centuries. The earliest surviving version was published in *Melismata. Musical phansies fitting the court, citie and countrey humours*, in 1611. These 'melismata' (a category of song) were collected by the English composer, musical editor and arranger Thomas Ravenscroft and organized under such headings as 'citie conceites' and 'country pastimes'. However, there are traces of similar songs dating back even further. A Scottish book from 1549 has one with the lyrics 'The frog cam to the myl dur'; and there was a 1580 ballad entitled 'A most Strange weddinge of the ffrogge and the mowse'.

The verses may have formed a kind of spinners' work song. The refrain quoted in *Melismata* – Humble-dum, humble-dum,/tweedle, tweedle, twino – is similar to several known spinning refrains, with 'humble-dum' evoking the humming of the spinning wheel and 'tweedle twino' suggesting the twiddling and twining of the thread as it is spun. In some variants of the song, the mouse herself is a spinner.

The 'rowley, powley' refrain does not appear before the nineteenth century, and the proposition that 'Rowley' was really Charles II, who lived two centuries earlier, seems improbable.

Bobby Shafto's Gone to Sea

Bobby Shafto's gone to sea,
Silver buckles at his knee;
He'll come back and marry me,
Bonny Bobby Shafto!

Bobby Shafto's bright and fair,
Panning out his yellow hair;
He's my love for evermore,
Bonny Bobby Shafto!

'Bobby Shafto' has been linked with a person of the same name who lived in County Wicklow in Ireland and died in 1737. However, the poem here has an even stronger connection with the northeast of England that goes back to the previous century and the traditional music of that part of the country: the tune to which the verses are normally sung is based on a Northumbrian one dating back to the 1690s. In those lyrics, 'Willy Foster' or 'Willie Forster' – not Bobby Shafto – is the man who goes to sea.

Another connection with the northeast is the real-life Bobby Shafto (sometimes spelt Shaftoe), an eighteenth-century Member of Parliament who was born and grew up in County Durham. Whether or not he was the original subject of the rhyme was immaterial to his supporters, who used the song in his campaign in the 1761 British general election, adding another verse:

Bobby Shafto's looking out,
All his ribbons flew about,
All the ladies gave a shout,
Hey for Boy Shafto!

This Shafto certainly was a looker – a portrait shows him as a young and handsome man with blond hair – and possibly a heartbreaker too.

❄ ❄ ❄

Curly-locks, Curly-locks

Curly-locks, Curly-locks,
Wilt thou be mine?
Thou shalt not wash the dishes,
Nor yet feed the swine;
But sit on a cushion,
And sew a fine seam
And feed upon strawberries,
Sugar, and cream.

A recent theory has it that the 'Curly-locks' of the rhyme was Charles II – certainly with his elaborate curly wig he fits the description – but there is no supporting evidence for this proposition. There are similar rhymes dating to the late eighteenth and early nineteenth centuries, and in her fascinating two-volume work, *The Traditional Games of England, Scotland and Ireland* (1894–8) the folklorist Alice

Bertha Gomme lists the verse as a children's song and game. She also quotes a version in the old Cumbrian dialect from the northwest of England:

> Bonny lass, canny lass,
> Wilta be mine?
> Thou's nowder wesh dishes
> Nor sarra the swine:
> But sit on thy crippy, etc.

The Cumbrian lass may not have had to 'sarra' (look after) the pigs but there's no soft seating on offer for this hardworking country girl: in the local dialect, 'crippy' is a four-legged stool.

Where Are You Going, My Pretty Maid?

> Where are you going, my pretty maid?
> I'm going a milking, sir, she said.
> May I go with you, my pretty maid?
> You're kindly welcome, sir, she said.
> What is your father, my pretty maid?
> My father's a farmer, sir, she said.
> What is your fortune, my pretty maid?
> My face is my fortune, sir, she said.
> Then I won't marry you, my pretty maid.
> Nobody asked you, sir, she said.

With its admirably sassy heroine, this is both a nursery rhyme and traditional English folk song. Its age and origins are difficult to pin down, but a Cornish version of the song lyrics appeared as long ago as 1790 in *Archaeologica Cornu-Britannica*, a grammar and dictionary written and compiled by William Pryce in an attempt to 'preserve the ancient Cornish language'. The first verse, which repeats the first two lines of the English version, reads:

> Pleth esos-sy ow mos mowes a vry? [Where are
>   you going, my pretty maid?]
> Pleth esos-sy ow mos mowes a vry? [Where are
>   you going, my pretty maid?]
> Yth af-vy dhe wodra yn-meth-hy, [I'm going a-
>   milking, sir, she said,
> yn-meth-hy, yn-meth-hy [Sir, she said, sir, she
>   said,
> Yth af-vy dhe wodra yn-meth-hy. [I'm going a-
>   milking, sir, she said.]

※※※

Matrimony

Fiddle-de-dee, Fiddle-de-dee

> Fiddle-de-dee, fiddle-de-dee,
> The fly has married the bumblebee.

114

They went to the church, and married was she:
The fly has married the bumblebee.

The Nursery Rhymes of England (1842), first recorded this rhyme. Other forms of the same narrative have been around a lot longer – the bumblebee's wedding is alluded to in another rhyme, which dates back to 1740:

A cat came dancing out of the barn,
With a fiddle under her arm.
She could play nothing but fiddle-cum-fee,
The mouse has married the bumble bee.

Sometimes a wasp replaces the fly, and in some versions the bee is referred to by its much older name, 'humble-bee', which can be traced back at least to fifteenth-century English – here 'humble' does not mean self-effacing but relates to the insect's humming.

Peter, Peter, Pumpkin Eater

Peter, Peter, pumpkin eater,
Had a wife and couldn't keep her;
He put her in a pumpkin shell
And there he kept her very well.

Peter, Peter, pumpkin eater,
Had another, and didn't love her;
Peter learned to read and spell,
And then he loved her very well.

Unlike the devoted fly from the previous rhyme, 'Peter' has matrimonial troubles and goes to extremes to solve them. The rhyme first made it onto the printed page in *Infant Institutes*, published in London in about 1797; in 1825, it popped up again in Boston in *Mother Goose's Quarto*. But in a version from Aberdeen in about 1868, Peter resorts to murder:

Peter, my neeper [neighbour?],
Had a wife,
And he couldna' keep her,
He pat her i' the wa',
And lat a' the mice eat her.

The verse above is thought to be an older version of the equally dark:

Eeper Weeper, chimney sweeper,
Had a wife but couldn't keep her.
Had another, didn't love her,
Up the chimney he did shove her.

116

EATING AND DRINKING

HISTORY BOOKS TELL us about the grand events of the past – the battles and conquests, the kings and queens – but it is the minutiae of the everyday world that really bring the past to life, particularly the culinary customs of ordinary people, which the rhymes here describe.

Come, Butter, Come

> Come, butter, come,
> Come, butter, come;
> Peter stands at the gate
> Waiting for his buttered cake;
> Come, butter, come.

For many centuries, this staple was produced by hand, by agitating cream or milk in a special butter churn. It was a tedious process, but it could be helped along by resorting to magic. Writing in *A Candle in the Dark: Or, A Treatise Concerning the*

Nature of Witches and Witchcraft in 1656, Thomas Ady described an old woman who insisted that she could churn milk to butter instantly by repeating the above rhyme three times. 'It was taught my Mother by a learned Church-man in Queen Maries days,' the old woman explained, 'when as Churchmen had more cunning and could teach people many a trick, that our Ministers now a days know not.'

The line 'Peter stands at the gate' refers to St Peter. Similar lines are found in other magical rhymes, like one beginning 'When Peter sat at Jerusalem's gate', designed to relieve toothache.

Do You Know the Muffin Man?

Do you know the muffin man,
The muffin man, the muffin man,
Do you know the muffin man,
Who lives on Drury Lane?

Yes, I know the muffin man,
The muffin man, the muffin man,
Yes, I know the muffin man,
Who lives on Drury Lane.

This rhyme conjures up cosy images of Victorian London, when freshly baked muffins were sold door to door by a 'muffin man', one of the many kinds of street trader. These would have been the plain, bread-like English muffins, rather than the American-style sweet cupcakes.

But we should have no equally comforting fantasies about Drury Lane. Today, the Lane borders fashionable Covent Garden, but back when the muffin man lived there the area was an appalling slum, peopled by thieves, pickpockets, drunks and prostitutes. The artist William Hogarth revealed the popular perceptions of it in his series of prints called *A Harlot's Progress* (1730–50), which shows scenes in and around Drury Lane.

Hot Cross Buns!

Hot cross buns!
Hot cross buns!
One a penny, two a penny,
Hot cross buns!

If you have no daughters,
Give them to your sons.
One a penny, two a penny,
Hot cross buns!

This is the familiar version of the rhyme, but there are two lesser-known lines that come at the end:

But if you haven't got any of these pretty little elves
You cannot do better than eat them yourselves.

Like many other rhymes, this was once a street cry called out by hawkers selling the hot cross buns that

SACRED BUNS

Some theorists say that hot cross buns have their origins in Greek and Roman times; others that they are the descendants of the small fruit-studded loaves baked by the Anglo-Saxons in honour of their spring goddess, Eostre. By the early seventeenth century in England, baked goods marked with a cross were seen as unacceptably 'Popish' by the Puritans, an austere Protestant group then in power. But buns thus decorated were acceptable if restricted to Good Friday, when they could be interpreted as commemorating the crucifixion of Christ on this day. The richness of the ingredients also marked the end of the preceding religious fast of Lent.

In folk tradition, hot cross buns baked on Good Friday would – like the immortal body of Christ – never decay, while the cross on top gave protection from evil spirits.

are traditionally eaten for breakfast on Good Friday. First recorded in 1797 in *The Newest Christmas Box* – a collection of songs with tunes by the English musician Reginald Spofforth – an earlier version of a similar street cry dates to 1733, printed in *Poor Robin's Almanack* (an almanac series produced by an unknown author under the pseudonym 'Poor Robin'):

> Good Friday comes this month, the old woman runs
> With one or two a penny hot cross buns.

The rhyme subsequently became the accompaniment to a game, in which children pile their hands one on top of each other in turn, in rhythm with the lines.

If All the World Were Paper

> If all the world were paper,
> And all the sea were ink,
> If all the trees were bread and cheese,
> What should we have to drink?

In circulation for at least four centuries, as far back as the reign of Charles I (1625–49), the apparent child-like innocence of this little rhyme belies its intent. In fact, it arose as a parody mocking the hyperbolic language used in ancient Jewish and medieval Christian passages; God's power and love were so immeasurable that all of creation was not large enough to contain them, as these words, translated by Rabbi Mayir ben Isaac in the eleventh or twelfth centuries, remind us:

> Could we with ink the ocean fill ...
> And were the skies of parchment made ...
> To tell the love of God alone
> Would drain the ocean dry ...

The Rabbi's translation entered English oral tradition, but still no words were adequate to describe God's boundless magnanimity, as this 1779 verse points out:

> Cou'd we with Ink the Ocean Fill;
> Was the whole Earth of Parchment made;
> Was every single stick a Quill;
> Was every Man a Scribe by Trade;
> To write the Love of God alone
> Would drain the Ocean dry;
> Nor wou'd the Scroll contain the Whole,
> Though Stretch'd from Sky to Sky.

Back in 1430, however, the English monk and poet John Lydgate took the opportunity to rework the well-known verse to compare the infinite universe not to the size of God's love but to the scale of female treachery. In 'A balade warning men to beware of deceitful women', he said:

122

In soth to saie, though all the yerth so wanne
Wer parchiment smoth, white and scribabell,
And the great se, that called is the Ocean,
Were tournid into ynke blackir than sabell,
Eche sticke a pen, eche man a scrivener abel,
Not coud thei writin woman's trechirie,
Beware therefore, the blind eteth many' a flie.

In modern English, this roughly translates as:

In truth to say, though all the earth so ashen
Were parchment smooth, white, and writable,
And the great sea, called ocean,
Were turned to ink, blacker than is sable,
Each stick a pen, each man a writer able,
They couldn't write women's treachery,
Beware therefore, the blind swallows many a fly.

I Had a Little Nut Tree

I had a little nut tree,
Nothing would it bear,
But a silver nutmeg
And a golden pear;

The King of Spain's daughter
Came to visit me,
And all for the sake
Of my little nut tree.

Nursery rhymes beginning 'I had' number at least twenty – it is, after all, a great opening line because almost anything can follow. These particular verses first made an appearance in print in 1797, in *The Newest Christmas Box*. However, in *The Nursery Rhymes of England* of 1842, the great nursery-rhyme collector James Orchard Halliwell suggests that they go back much further and that the king's daughter mentioned here was actually Juana of Castile (1479–1555) – commonly known as *La Loca*, or Joanna the Mad. Juana did visit Henry VIII in 1506 but, apart from this snippet of information, there is little evidence to support Halliwell's proposition, so we are left guessing.

The first two verses are the most familiar ones but, in 1853, Halliwell recorded a third:

I skipp'd over water,
I danced over sea,
And all the birds in the air
Couldn't catch me.

There are a further two, later, additions to the rhyme, but these take us even further from the idea of Juana as the 'King of Spain's daughter': like her sister Katherine of Aragon, first wife to Henry VIII, Juana did not have 'jet black' but reddish hair:

Her dress was made of crimson,
Jet black was her hair,
She asked me for my nutmeg
And my golden pear.

I said, 'So fair a princess
Never did I see,
I'll give you all the fruit
From my little nut tree.'

Jack Sprat Could Eat No Fat

Jack Sprat could eat no fat.
His wife could eat no lean.
And so between the two of them,
They licked the platter clean.

In his 1639 collection of proverbs for children, *Paroemiologia Anglo-Latina*, John Clarke offers the following:

Jack will eat not fat, and Jill doth love no leane.
Yet betwixt them both they lick the dishes cleane.

'Jack Prat' and the later form 'Jack Sprat' were sixteenth- and seventeenth-century terms for an abnormally small person. Perhaps lampooning a cleric of particularly diminutive stature, James

Howell's 1659 *Proverbs, or old Sayed Sawes & Adages* reworked the rhyme thus:

> Archdeacon Pratt would eat no fatt,
> His wife would eat no lean;
> Twixt Archdeacon Pratt, and Joan his wife,
> The meat was eat up clean.

The rhyme shows up again, in the form we know today, in John Ray's *English Proverbs* in 1670. Nineteenth-century chapbooks pick up the story of Jack and his wife with additional verses such as:

> Jack Sprat
> Had a cat,
> It had but one ear;
> It went to buy butter
> When butter was dear.

Pat-a-cake, Pat-a-cake, Baker's Man

> Pat-a-cake, pat-a-cake, baker's man.
> Bake me a cake as fast as you can.
> Pat it, and prick it, and mark it with 'B'
> And put it in the oven for baby and me!

This jolly jingle – or at least something resembling it – made its first appearance as far back as 1698 in the play *The Campaigners*, a satirical comedy by Tom D'Urfey, where the latter's 'affected tattling nurse' babbles it to the child she is suckling. Nearly seventy years later, in about 1765, *Mother Goose's Melody* recorded a rhyme more akin to the modern one:

> Patty Cake, Patty Cake,
> Baker's Man;
> That I will Master,
> As fast as I can;
> Prick it and prick it,
> And mark it with a T,
> And there will be enough for Jackey and me.

In the days before households had their own ovens, it's conceivable that pies, breads and other baked goods really were marked with a letter. Unable to bake at home, people took items to the baker, who would bake them in a communal oven. Marking your pie or bread with a letter would have been a way of ensuring that you got the correct item back.

In the nineteenth century, children recited the lines of this rhyme in time to a clapping game, using different actions to mime what is happening in each stage of the verse.

Pease Porridge Hot

> Pease porridge hot,
> Pease porridge cold,
> Pease porridge in the pot,
> Nine days old.
>
> Some like it hot,
> Some like it cold,
> Some like it in the pot,
> Nine days old.

Pease porridge, also known as pease pudding, is a traditional British dish consisting of a thick purée of split yellow peas, flavoured with seasoning and herbs. This is real comfort food and is often accompanied by a joint of gammon or ham.

The rhyme was first published in 1797, in the *Newest Christmas Box*. Like 'Pat-a-cake' (see page 126), the snappy lines form the basis of a children's clapping game.

'Nine days old' is a refrain that is not unique to these verses: it occurs elsewhere, for example, in the street cry:

> Mince pies hot,
> Mince pies cold,
> Mince pies in addition
> Nine days old.

The significance of this specific number of days is not known; it may purely have been used for dramatic effect, because even the poorest, who would top up the pot with scraps, would be too hungry to leave food for that long.

❦

Polly Put the Kettle On

Polly put the kettle on,
Polly put the kettle on,
Polly put the kettle on,
We'll all have tea.

Sukey take it off again,
Sukey take it off again,
Sukey take it off again,
They've all gone away.

If you know this rhyme you will almost certainly know the tune to which it is sung, for the two are inseparable – so inseparable, in fact, that it's impossible to launch into the words without singing them. The tune itself comes from a Scottish country dance called 'Jenny's Bawbee', which has been known since at least the 1770s. The rhyming of 'tea' with 'away' works only if the former is pronounced the Old English way as 'tay', which suggests that the rhyme has been in existence a long time.

'Polly' and 'Sukey' may really have been 'Mary' and 'Susan', for in the mid-eighteenth century these were the pet forms of the latter names – and in variations dating from around 1800 'Polly' changes into 'Molly'. The first time the rhyme as we know it appeared in print was in 1814, when Charles Dickens mentioned it in his novel *Barnaby Rudge*.

There is also an additional, lesser-known third verse:

Blow the fire
And make the toast,
Put the muffins down to roast,
Blow the fire and make the toast,
We'll all have tea.

The Queen of Hearts

The Queen of Hearts
She made some tarts,
All on a summer's day;
The Knave of Hearts
He stole those tarts,
And took them clean away.

The King of Hearts
Called for the tarts,

And beat the knave full sore;
The Knave of Hearts
Brought back the tarts,
And vowed he'd steal no more.

Queen, King and Knave of Hearts – these characters clearly come from the suit of hearts in a deck of playing cards. The rhyme first appeared in April 1782 in *The European Magazine*, a monthly literary, cultural and political journal published in London, along with further verses about the King of Clubs, the King of Spades and the Diamond King. Only 'The Queen of Hearts' remained popular, however, and this verse has survived, while the others have vanished into obscurity. Indeed, it has been argued that 'The Queen of Hearts' was the original composition and that the others were later additions.

WHAT DOES IT MEAN?

It has, of course, been tempting to speculate as to whether this queen was modelled on a real monarch. French playing cards from the mid-seventeenth century depict the Jewish queen Judith as the Queen of Hearts. Elizabeth of Bohemia (1596–1662), daughter of King James I of England and VI of Scotland, has also been proposed because her beauty, charm and courage earned her the nickname 'Queen of Hearts'.

Sing a Song of Sixpence

Sing a song of sixpence,
A pocket full of rye.
Four and twenty blackbirds,
Baked in a pie.

When the pie was opened
The birds began to sing;
Wasn't that a dainty dish,
To set before the king.

The king was in his counting house,
Counting out his money;
The queen was in the parlour,
Eating bread and honey.

The maid was in the garden,
Hanging out the clothes,
When down came a blackbird
And pecked off her nose.

This nursery rhyme has been linked to Henry James Pye who, in 1790, was appointed Poet Laureate and set about writing his first poem in honour of the king's birthday. With allusions to feathered songsters, it was a poor effort and the Shakespearean scholar George Steevens quickly responded with a pun on the Laureate's name: 'And when the PYE was opened, the birds began to sing; Was not that a dainty dish to set before the king?'

It's an amusing story – but untrue. A version of the first verse had already made an appearance in print nearly fifty years earlier, in 1744, in *Tommy Thumb's Pretty Song Book*:

Sing a Song of Sixpence,
A bag full of Rye,
Four and twenty Naughty Boys,
Baked in a Pye.

A 1780 variant replaced the Naughty Boys with birds, and in 1784 *Gammer Gurton's Garland* changed the offending bird in the last verse to a magpie instead of a blackbird.

WHAT DOES IT MEAN?

All sorts of wild and wonderful theories abound as to the meaning of this rhyme: the blackbirds represent the hours of the day – or the monasteries that are about to be offered up to Henry VIII as a dainty pie – or they are the letters of the alphabet in the first printing of the Bible in English (rather than Latin). The final blackbird is a devil snapping off the maid's nose to reach her soul; the king symbolizes the sun; the queen personifies the moon.

In all these attempts to interpret the rhyme, one obvious detail has been overlooked: songbirds were (and are) eaten, and one particular amusement was

SIXTEENTH-CENTURY BAKE-OFF

Epulario, an Italian cookery book dating from 1549, explains exactly how 'to make pies so that the birds may be alive in them and flie out when it is cut up'. Here is a translation:

Make the coffin of a great pie or pastry, in the bottome thereof make a hole as big as your fist, or bigger if you will, let the sides of the coffin bee somewhat higher then ordinary pies, which done put it full of flower and bake it, and being baked, open the hole in the bottome, and take out the flower. Then having a pie of the bigness of the hole in the bottome of the coffin aforesaid, you shal put it into the coffin, withall put into the said coffin round about the aforesaid pie as many small live birds as the empty coffin will hold, besides the pie aforesaid. And this is to be done at such time as you send the pie to the table, and set before the guests: where uncovering or cutting up the lid of the great pie, all the birds will flie out, which is to delight and pleasure shew to the company.

to encase live birds underneath a pastry lid, which, when the pastry was cut, would fly out.

Christmas

Christmas Is Coming

> Christmas is coming and the goose is getting fat,
> Please put a penny in the old man's hat;
> If you haven't got a penny, a ha'penny will do;
> If you haven't got a ha'penny, then God bless you!

This rhyme is traditionally sung to the English folk tune 'Country Gardens', but some well-known names have recorded versions of it too, for example the folk group The Kingston Trio, country singer John Denver and none other than Bing Crosby.

The reference to a goose dates back to the time when goose, not turkey, was the centrepiece of the Christmas table. The image of the old beggar asking for charity at Christmastime is still familiar to us today: this is the season of giving, especially since the rest of the year may be a lot leaner, as this familiar proverb, printed in John Clarke's *Paroemiologia Latina* in 1639, suggests:

> Christmas comes but once a year
> And when it comes it brings good cheer.

Dame, Get Up and Bake Your Pies

Dame, get up and bake your pies,
Bake your pies, bake your pies;
Dame, get up and bake your pies,
On Christmas day in the morning.

Dame, what makes your maidens lie,
Maidens lie, maidens lie;
Dame, what makes your maidens lie,
On Christmas day in the morning?

Dame, what makes your ducks to die,
Ducks to die, ducks to die;
Dame, what makes your ducks to die,
On Christmas day in the morning?

These three verses are the first of four that form the lyrics to a song and carol that was widely known by the late eighteenth century. An 1823 edition of the *Gentleman's Magazine* printed the first two lines.

The pies that the dame is tasked with baking may have been mince pies – but she may also have added minced meat to the familiar fruit filling, as was the custom prior to the mid-nineteenth century. Echoes of this remain in the beef suet that still forms part of the traditional mixture.

TALKING ANIMALS

Beatrix Potter, that lover of nursery rhymes, alludes to the rhyme in *The Tailor of Gloucester*. In the magic time between Christmas Eve and Christmas morning, so the story tells us, 'all the beasts can talk'. On this particular night, it continues, 'From all the roofs and gables and old wooden houses in Gloucester came a thousand merry voices singing the old Christmas rhymes ... First and loudest the cocks cried out: "Dame, get up, and bake your pies!"'

Flour of England, Fruit of Spain

Flour of England, fruit of Spain,
Met together in a shower of rain;
Put in a bag, tied round with a string,
If you tell me this riddle,
I'll give you a ring.

The generally accepted answer to this riddle is: plum pudding or, as it is more commonly known now, Christmas pudding, as typically graces the British Christmas table. There are no actual plums in the recipe, 'plum' once being the generic name for raisins and other dried fruit. Traditionally, the pudding mix was wrapped up in a pudding cloth, secured with string, and boiled – hence all those old pictures of perfectly round Christmas puddings.

But another theory suggests that the verse has a deeper meaning. In her scholarly study of 1930, *The Real Personages of Mother Goose*, Katherine Elwes Thomas argues that the rhyme was current at the time of the Tudor Queen Mary – the 'flower of England' – who was proposing to marry the Spanish Philip II – the 'fruit of Spain'. A contemporary account records that their first meeting took place in a downpour – 'met together in a shower of rain'. And 'I'll give you a ring' could refer to the ring that Mary sent Philip to symbolize their marriage.

CHAPTER 8

THE
NATURAL WORLD

RAIN AND WIND are not welcome, even in nursery rhymes, but the moon and stars are another matter. Apart from the eccentric lunar inhabitants in two of the rhymes here, the moon and stars are to be revered, for they have the magical power to protect and to grant wishes.

Weather-watchers

Dr Foster Went to Gloucester

> Doctor Foster went to Gloucester
> In a shower of rain;
> He stepped in a puddle,
> Right up to his middle,
> And never went there again.

Although this rhyme was not recorded until the 1844 edition of *The Nursery Rhymes of England*, the pairing of 'middle' with 'puddle' indicates that the archaic form 'piddle' may originally have been used, suggesting that the verse is older. The 1810 edition

139

of *Gammer Gurton's Garland* gives a slightly earlier variant:

> Old Dr Foster went to Gloster,
> To preach the word of God.
> When he came there, he sat in his chair,
> And gave all the people a nod.

One theory proposes that the doctor was, in reality, the English king Edward I (1239–1307), who once visited Gloucester and whose horse got so stuck in the mud there that the monarch refused to visit the city ever again. Other suggestions are that he was an envoy sent to Gloucester by William Laud, Archbishop of Canterbury (1573–1645), or even that there is a connection with the play *Doctor Faustus* by Christopher Marlowe (1564–93), in which the eponymous doctor is referred to as 'Doctor Fauster'. Since the rhyme was not recorded until the nineteenth century, however, these interpretations can only be speculative.

It's Raining, It's Pouring

> It's raining, it's pouring.
> The old man is snoring.
> He went to bed and bumped his head,
> And couldn't get up in the morning.

This is one version of the rhyme, but in others the 'old man' is replaced by 'old woman' or 'children'. Just the first two lines appeared in print in 1912, in *The Little Mother Goose*, published in the United States. The tune to which the words are usually sung is the same as for 'A-tisket, A-tasket' (I've lost my yellow basket). Twenty-seven years later, in 1939, the American folklorist Herbert Halpert made the first-known audio recording of the song.

One particularly dark interpretation of the rhyme is that it refers to an accidental death after a head injury: 'bumped his head and couldn't get up in the morning'.

Rain, Rain, Go Away

Rain, rain, go away,
Come again another day.

In 1687, the English antiquary and writer John Aubrey observed: 'Little children have a custome when it raines to sing, or charme away the Raine; thus they all joine in a chorus and sing thus ...

Raine, raine, goe away,
Come againe a Saterday.

'I have a conceit,' Aubrey continues, 'that this childish custom is of Great Antiquity ...' Aubrey may well have been right for it seems that children have been chanting this fair-weather invocation for generations, even as far back as ancient Greece – if not exactly in this form. In his *Proverbs* of 1659, James Howell had already recorded the following: 'Raine, raine, goe to Spain: faire weather come againe.'

VARYING THE THEME

The simplicity of the rhyme allows infinite variations, depending on one's purpose, be it ... practical:

Rain, rain, go to Spain,
Never show your face again.

Rain, rain, come down and pour,
Then you'll only last an hour.

Rain, rain, go away,
Come again on April/Midsummer/Washing day.

... egocentric:

Rain, rain, go away,
Little Arthur/Johnny wants to play.

Rain, rain, pour down,
But not a drop on our town.

Rain on the green grass, and rain on the tree,
And rain on the housetop, but not on me.

... or just plain spiteful:

Rain, rain, go away,
Come on Martha's wedding day.

❦

The North Wind Doth Blow

The north wind doth blow,
And we shall have snow,
And what will the robin do then?
Poor thing.
He'll sit in a barn,
And keep himself warm,
And hide his head under his wing.
Poor thing.

Not much can be said about the origins of this verse, which so evocatively conjures the chill of winter, other than that it goes back more than two hundred years. It was first published in 1805 in *Songs for the Nursery*, a treasury that celebrates the nursery rhyme. 'The rapid advances made by the principle of "Utility" in the modern system of education,' the book asserts, 'have not been able to push into oblivion the Nursery Rhymes of our forefathers ...

but this we know for ourselves, that we love them, and have ever loved them, since we listened to them on our nurse's knee.'

The rhyme appeared again in various books throughout the nineteenth century, as well as in *Mother Goose*, illustrated by Arthur Rackham, in 1913.

✿ ❋ ✿

Stargazers

I See the Moon

> I see the moon,
> And the moon sees me;
> God bless the moon,
> And God bless me.

First recorded back in 1784 in *Gammer Gurton's Garland*, this simple rhyme demonstrates children's fascination with the moon. When it is new, they traditionally bow to it; when it is full, they see a face in it; and in this and similar rhymes, they call on it. An old Lancashire version goes:

> I see the moon,
> And the moon sees me;
> God bless the priest
> That christened me.

Fishermen's children had their own variant:

I see the moon,
And the moon sees me;
God bless the sailors
On the sea.

Twentieth-century American children recited:

I see the moon,
The moon sees me;
The moon sees somebody
I want to see.

And in Yorkshire, children's nurses said:

Moon penny bright as silver,
Come and play with little childer.

❄ ✳ ❄

Star Light, Star Bright

Star light, star bright,
First star I see tonight;
I wish I may, I wish I might,
Have the wish I wish tonight.

This short rhyme is thought to be of American origin and to date from the late nineteenth century. But what it refers to is a lot older: the ancient belief in the magical power and significance of stars.

1. The first star that shines at night was thought to be particularly potent. Gazing at it and making a wish as you did so guaranteed that your wish would come true.

2. Just seeing a shooting star as it fell was said to bring good luck – but for good measure, it was better to make a specific wish as you watched it falling.

꧁ ✳ ꧂

The Man in the Moon

> The man in the moon
> Came down too soon,
> And asked his way to Norwich;
> He went by the south,
> And burnt his mouth
> With supping cold pease porridge.

Gammer Gurton's Garland of 1784 was the first to print this rhyme, but offers a different last line: 'With supping hot pease porridge'. By 1805, *Songs for the Nursery* had changed the line to 'With eating cold plum-porridge', and turned the Man in the Moon to 'the man in the South'. It has been suggested that the subject of the verse refers to the nineteenth-century 'man in the moon', a slang term for someone who negotiated bribes at election time. This is unlikely, however, because the rhyme was known earlier.

The figure of the Man in the Moon is traditionally depicted with a lantern and a bush of thorns, as in this seventeenth-century ballad in which he is partial to the odd tipple:

> The man in the Moon drinks Clarret,
> With Powder-beef, Turnep, and Carret.
> A Cup of old Malago Sack
> Will fire his bush at his back.

Just how the man got to be in the moon in the first place is explained in this variant, in which he prevents worshippers from attending church by scattering thorns in their path; in consequence, he is banished to the moon:

> The Man in the Moon was caught in a trap
> For stealing the thorns from another man's gap.
> If he had gone by, and let the thorns lie,
> He'd never been Man in the Moon so high.

PORRIDGE OR PUDDING?

Clues to the origins and age of a rhyme can often be glimpsed in individual words. As one astute culinary observer noted, if the 'plum porridge' mentioned here was the original wording, the rhyme must predate the time when plum pudding – the Christmas pudding of the British festive table – replaced the older dish.

A recipe from around 1420 describes plum porridge, or 'pottage', as a thick soup or stew made with veal, mutton or chicken, thickened with bread, coloured with red sandalwood, and filled with currants. By the time of Elizabeth I (1533–1603), this mixture, 'made thick with meate or crummes of bread' as one 1573 recipe describes it, had another ingredient: prunes. These dried plums became so popular that 'plum' became a generic term for all dried fruits (see 'Flour of England, Fruit of Spain', page 137).

By the end of the eighteenth century, plum porridge had almost entirely disappeared, to be replaced by its relative, the plum pudding – without the meat, but still retaining the breadcrumbs, animal fat (suet) and dried fruit.

There Was a Man Lived in the Moon

There was a man lived in the moon, lived in the
   moon, lived in the moon,
There was a man lived in the moon,
And his name was Aiken Drum.
And he played upon a ladle, a ladle, a ladle,
And he played upon a ladle,
And his name was Aiken Drum.

And his hat was made of good cream cheese, of
   good cream cheese, of good cream cheese,
And his hat was made of good cream cheese,
And his name was Aiken Drum.

And his coat was made of good roast beef, of good
   roast beef, of good roast beef,
And his coat was made of good roast beef,
And his name was Aiken Drum.

And his buttons were made of penny loaves,
   of penny loaves, of penny loaves,
And his buttons were made of penny loaves,
 And his name was Aiken Drum.

And his waistcoat was made of crust pies, of crust
   pies, of crust pies,
And his waistcoat was made of crust pies,
And his name was Aiken Drum.

And his breeches were made of haggis bags, of
  haggis bags, of haggis bags,
And his breeches were made of haggis bags,
And his name was Aiken Drum.

The origins of this rhyme remain a mystery, other than that it was known in Scotland in 1821 (the haggis bags are a clue) when it was printed in a collection of Scottish songs and legends called *The Jacobite Relics of Scotland*.

The name 'Aikendrum' was also mentioned in an old ballad about the Battle of Sheriffmuir. This took place in 1715 near Dunblane in Scotland. On one side were the Jacobites, supporters of the Scottish Catholic House of Stuart and opposers of the Act of Union of 1707 that united Scotland and England; on the other side were forces loyal to the English Crown and George I, of the German Protestant House of Hanover, who took the British throne in 1714. The 'Whig' in the song was a member of a political party that supported the Hanoverians:

Ken you how a Whig can fight,
Aikendrum, Aikendrum?
Ken you how a Whig can fight,
Aikendrum?

Twinkle, Twinkle, Little Star

Twinkle, twinkle, little star,
How I wonder what you are!
Up above the world so high,
Like a diamond in the sky.

When the blazing sun is gone,
When he nothing shines upon,
Then you show your little light,
Twinkle, twinkle, through the night.

Then the traveller in the dark
Thanks you for your tiny spark;
He could not see which way to go,
If you did not twinkle so.

In the dark blue sky you keep,
And often through my curtains peep,
For you never shut your eye
'Till the sun is in the sky.

As your bright and tiny spark
Lights the traveller in the dark,
Though I know not what you are,
Twinkle, twinkle, little star.

One of the best known of all English-language nursery rhymes, this is still widely sung to young children today. However, only the first verse is familiar and it is surprising to discover that there are four more. Unlike so many other nursery rhymes that need interpretive unpicking and have obscure origins, there are no hidden meanings here. This poem is about exactly what it says it's about – a small star shining in the night sky.

We know its provenance too: it was written by Jane Taylor (1783–1824), under the title 'The Star', and published in 1806 in *Rhymes for the Nursery*. The book was a collaborative work with Jane's sister Ann, and was hugely successful. 'The Star' – or the first verse at any rate – moved from the printed page into oral tradition, so that now we know it by heart, even though we may not remember its creator.

The rhyme's familiar tune is based on an old French song '*Ah, vous dirai-je, Maman*', on which Mozart subsequently based twelve variations.

CHAPTER 9

JOURNEYS AND PLACES

MANY OF THE verses that follow were singing rhymes that accompanied children's games, or even old dances, which explains why some are so long. Some offer a wonderful travelogue to places that still exist, thus linking the past with the present.

How Many Miles to Babylon?

How many miles to Babylon?
Three score miles and ten.
Can I get there by candle-light?
Yes, and back again.
If your heels are nimble and your toes are light,
You may get there by candle-light.

These strange and magical words once accompanied a children's singing game, but the verse has since survived purely as a nursery rhyme. 'Babylon' may be a corruption of 'babyland', but more probably alludes to the imagined city of that name used in the seventeenth century – a sort of archetypal fantasy metropolis that exemplified everything exotic, faraway and fabulous. The saying 'Can I get there by candle-light?' was familiar back in Elizabethan times, suggesting that the references in the rhyme – if not the rhyme itself – go back a long way.

With 'Cantelon' as a corruption of Caledon (Caledonia, or Scotland), a Scottish version runs:

> King and Queen of Cantelon,
> How many miles to Babylon?
> Eight and eight, and other eight.
> Will I get there by candle-light?
> If your horse be good and your spurs be bright.
> How mony men have ye?
> Mae nae ye daur come and see. [More than of any you dare come and see.]

London Bridge Is Falling Down

> London Bridge is falling down,
> Falling down, falling down.
> London Bridge is falling down,
> My fair lady.

This is the first and most familiar verse of a rhyme that, like others here, was once the accompaniment to a game. The second verse offers a solution …

Build it up with wood and clay,
Wood and clay, wood and clay,
Build it up with wood and clay,
My fair lady.

… which is immediately dispelled by the third verse:

Wood and clay will wash away,
Wash away, wash away,
Wood and clay will wash away,
My fair lady.

Following the same form, successive verses come up with other options:

- Bricks and mortar – but these 'will not stay'.
- Iron and steel – but these will 'bend and bow'.
- Silver and gold – but these will 'be stolen away'.

Finally, it is suggested that a man be set to watch all night to guard against the malevolent forces causing the bridge's collapse. To stop him falling asleep, it is advised that he be given a pipe to smoke.

The earliest English text that most closely resembles the modern rhyme appeared in *Tommy*

THE REAL LONDON BRIDGE

There have been bridges over the River Thames in London since Roman times; the London Bridge of nursery-rhyme fame is said to date to 1176, when construction began on a new stone-arched bridge to replace the previous wooden one. But this wasn't just a means of crossing the river: it was a shopping precinct and residential site combined. Shops lined either side of the roadway, with houses above the shops. By 1358, 138 premises were said to exist there, and in the 1580s, water mills were added too.

Despite disasters such as major fires and the collapse of some stone arches, as well as its general state of disrepair, London Bridge was the only crossing over the Thames until 1750, when Westminster Bridge opened.

Thumb's Pretty Song Book of 1744. But collapsing structures were not confined to London; bridges were falling apart all over Europe as far back as the Middle Ages, it seems – in France, Germany, Scandinavia and Hungary, and even across the Atlantic in Pennsylvania – if only in children's songs and games.

London's Burning

London's burning, London's burning.
Fetch the engines, fetch the engines.
Fire fire, fire fire!
Pour on water, pour on water.

As if the crumbling bridge in the last rhyme isn't enough, this verse has the capital city going down in flames. The city did indeed suffer a huge conflagration known as the Great Fire of London in the seventeenth century. It began on 2 September 1666 in a baker's shop in Pudding Lane. Fanned by a strong east wind, the flames quickly spread across the densely packed and highly flammable buildings; constructed from wood, covered with pitch and roofed with thatch, they provided perfect fuel. By the time the fire was finally extinguished, 13,200 houses, 87 churches, the Guildhall, the Royal Exchange and the medieval

St Paul's Cathedral were lost, along with many lives (despite the popular myth that only six died). However, there was no organized firefighting service at the time, and certainly no 'engines', so the wording itself cannot date from that time.

A similar verse called 'Scotland's Burning' is said to refer to the burning of Edinburgh in 1544, ordered by the English king, Henry VIII.

Oranges and Lemons

Oranges and lemons
Say the bells of St Clement's.

You owe me five farthings,
Say the bells of St Martin's.

When will you pay me?
Say the bells of Old Bailey.

When I grow rich,
Say the bells of Shoreditch.

When will that be?
Say the bells of Stepney.

I'm sure I don't know,
Says the great bell at Bow.

Here comes a candle to light you to bed,
Here comes a chopper to chop off your head.

One of the most famous of all nursery rhymes, this accompanies a children's game in which two children form an arch by joining hands; as they chant the rhyme the other players pass under the arch one by one; when the pair reach the last line, they bring their arms down around whoever is passing under the arch at that moment to 'chop off their head'. The game sometimes ends in a tug of war.

The last line has given rise to various interpretations; for example, that it evokes the days of public executions when the condemned were led to the place of execution to the tolling of bells. Others suggest that they refer to the six marriages of Henry VIII and the beheadings of some of his wives. However, the earliest recording of the rhyme, in *Tom Thumb's Pretty Song Book* (1744), makes no mention of heads being chopped off, so these theories seem unlikely.

CITY GUIDE

Other English towns and counties have laid claim to the rhyme by inserting the names of their own churches, but it is London churches that appear in the most famous form of the rhyme, which provides a travelogue to the old city. All the churches are said to be in, or just outside, the City of London, the oldest part of the metropolis:

- St Clement's, Eastcheap, and St Clement Danes could both be the church that rings out 'oranges and lemons'; the former lies near the wharves on the Thames where imported citrus fruit was once unloaded.
- St Martin's probably refers to St Martin's Lane in the City, the home of the moneylenders.
- St Sepulchre-without-Newgate, opposite the Old Bailey, is near the Fleet Prison where debtors were held.
- St Leonard's, Shoreditch, lies just outside the old demolished city walls.
- St Dunstan's, Stepney, is also outside the city walls.
- Bow is probably St Mary-le-Bow in Cheapside, whose bells rang out to tell Dick Whittington to 'turn again, Whittington, Lord Mayor of London'; to be a true Cockney – the traditional Londoner – you must have been born within the sound of Bow bells.

A longer version of the rhyme, in the 1810 edition of *Gammer Gurton's Garland*, lists even more London churches, beginning with the verse:

> Gay go up and gay go down,
> To ring the bells of London town.

Pop Goes the Weasel

There are many different versions of the lyrics to the song. In England, most share the basic verse:

Half a pound of tuppenny rice,
Half a pound of treacle.
That's the way the money goes,
Pop! goes the weasel.

Often a second verse is added, which may be any of the following:

Every night when I go out,
The monkey's on the table,
Take a stick and knock it off,
Pop! goes the weasel.

Up and down the city road,
In and out the Eagle.
That's the way the money goes,
Pop! goes the weasel.

'Round and 'round the cobbler's bench
The monkey chased the weasel,
The monkey thought 'twas all in fun.
Pop! goes the weasel.

A penny for a spool of thread,
A penny for a needle,
That's the way the money goes,
Pop! goes the weasel.

It seems that this originated as a dance tune to which words were later added. It was known in the nineteenth century in Britain, when it was played in dance halls and on barrel organs in the street. In the same century, it crossed the Atlantic to the United States, where it was known as 'the latest English dance'. There were numerous variations on the American lyrics, such as this, printed in 1858 in Boston:

> All around the cobbler's house,
> The monkey chased the people.
> And after them in double haste,
> Pop! goes the weasel.

A 1901 version from New York began:

> All around the chicken coop,
> The possum chased the weasel.

In Britain the words have accompanied a children's singing game since at least the late nineteenth century. As to the meaning of the words, the following theories have been put forward:

- 'Weasel' is a name for a yarn-measuring device used by weavers that makes a popping sound when the correct length has been counted.
- 'Weasel and stoat' is Cockney rhyming slang (a dialect spoken by indigenous Londoners) for 'coat'; 'pop' is slang for 'pawn', so could the

line refer to pawning your coat? 'Monkey' is also Cockney slang for £500 and there is still a pub called The Eagle on London's City Road, so this theory begins to sound appealing: perhaps you have to pawn your coat to pay off your drinking debts and other expenses?

Ride a Cock-horse to Banbury Cross

> Ride a cock-horse to Banbury Cross,
> To see a fine lady upon a white horse;
> Rings on her fingers and bells on her toes,
> And she shall have music wherever she goes.

This is the most familiar modern form of the rhyme, but in some older eighteenth-century versions the fine lady has morphed into an old woman and the horse has changed colour from white to black. *Tom Tit's Song Book*, of around 1790, describes her thus:

> A ring on her finger,
> A bonnet of straw,
> The strangest old woman
> That ever you saw.

Literary detectives have cited a number of potential clues in the wording as to the identity of the rider and the location and age of the rhyme:

- The bells on her toes suggest that the rider was a fifteenth-century fashionista, for the style then was to wear a bell on the pointed toe of each shoe.
- The market cross in Banbury, Oxfordshire, was destroyed at the end of the sixteenth century, but the site will have retained its memory.
- Other similar rhymes propose Shrewsbury Cross or Coventry Cross as the location, both in the English Midlands.
- A 'cock-horse' was a descriptive term for a high-spirited steed; it was also the name for a toy hobby horse (or, failing that, an adult's knee), which a child could straddle. (William Gladstone, one of Britain's most famous prime ministers, who served under Queen Victoria, used to sing the song to his children every day while they 'galloped' on his leg.)
- The fine lady may have been medieval noblewoman Lady Godiva who, according to legend, rode naked through the streets of Coventry in protest at the onerous taxes that her husband levied from his tenants; her modesty was protected by her cloak of long hair shrouding her form.

❧ ✳ ❧

TONGUE TWISTERS AND RIDDLING RHYMES

THE RHYMES THAT follow are just pure fun, and will tax the tongues and brains of adults just as much as those of children.

Twisters

Betty Botter Bought Some Butter

Betty Botter bought some butter,
But, she said, the butter's bitter;
If I put it in my batter
It will make my batter bitter,
But, a bit of better butter
Will make my batter better.
So she bought a bit of butter
Better than her bitter butter,
And she put it in her batter
And the batter was not bitter.
So t'was better Betty Botter bought a bit of better
butter.

Written by the American writer and poet Carolyn Wells, this first appeared in a book of her nonsense rhymes and poems called *The Jingle Book*, which was published in 1899. The familiar modern version above, recorded in 1934, differs only slightly from Wells's original.

Tongue twisters like this rely on alliteration and rapid repetition of similar sounds to challenge a person's ability to pronounce the words without getting tangled up in them. They can be used to help improve pronunciation.

Peter Piper Picked a Peck of Pickled Pepper

Peter Piper picked a peck of pickled pepper;
A peck of pickled pepper Peter Piper picked;
If Peter Piper picked a peck of pickled pepper,
Where's the peck of pickled peppers Peter Piper
    picked?

This well-known tongue twister has proved useful for drama students as an exercise to help them articulate their words better. It's also been recommended as a treatment for hiccups – provided it is repeated three times within one breath. It was first printed in *Peter Piper's Practical Principles of Plain and Perfect Pronunciation*, published in 1819, but may have been known a generation earlier.

SPICE SMUGGLER

As to the identity of 'Peter Piper', one theory points to Pierre Poivre, whose name translates into English as 'Peter Pepper'. Monsieur Poivre was an eighteenth-century French horticulturalist and government administrator. At the time, the lucrative trade in spices such as cloves, cinnamon and nutmeg was under the monopoly of the Dutch East India Company. The Dutch guarded their treasure well: they soaked nutmegs in lime juice to prevent them sprouting anywhere other than in Dutch-held territory – perhaps the origin of the 'pickled' pepper – and seeds for other spices were not available. But, while in the Far East, Poivre hit on a plan. With the support of the French East India Company, he smuggled spice plants out from under the noses of the Dutch and tried to grow them commercially in the French colonies of Mauritius and Réunion. His attempt failed, but he did establish a botanical garden on Mauritius, which still exists today, now known as the Sir Seewoosagur Ramgoolam Botanic Garden.

Riddles

As I Was Going to St Ives

As I was going to St Ives,
I met a man with seven wives,
Each wife had seven sacks,
Each sack had seven cats,
Each cat had seven kits:
Kits, cats, sacks, and wives,
How many were there going to St Ives?

How many of us have been tricked into thinking that complex maths is needed to answer the question in the last line? But re-read the verse carefully and we see that that the rhymer says nothing about being *accompanied* by any of this throng. The only person we can confidently say is headed for St Ives is the rhymer themself. So there is only one possible answer: one.

A form of this rhyme, which refers to nine rather than seven wives, was first published in about 1730, but the more familiar version appeared in 1825. There are two contenders for the destination: St Ives in Cornwall, once a busy fishing port, and the market town of St Ives in Cambridgeshire.

Old Mother Twitchett Has But One Eye

> Old Mother Twitchett has but one eye,
> And a long tail which she can let fly,
> And every time she goes over a gap,
> She leaves a bit of her tail in a trap.

Forget all thoughts of some one-eyed old biddy with a skeletal deformity – this is a riddle that needs decoding before you can find the answer. And the answer, of course, is: a needle and thread, the needle being Old Mother Twitchett herself and the thread being her tail.

In 1600, clever minds were challenged with a similar cryptic brainteaser:

> What is it that goes through thicke and thin
> And draws his guts after him?

The answer was: 'It is an Needle that goeth through thicke and thin cloth, drawing the thred after it, which is taken for the guts.'

Thirty White Horses

Thirty white horses
Upon a red hill,
Now they tramp,
Now they champ,
Now they stand still.

Another riddle that does not pose a question directly but presents it as a visual metaphor. Answer? The thirty white horses are the teeth, crunching, chewing and chomping up and down; and the red hill is the gum, or gums, to which they are attached.

The rhyme goes back to 1645. Another similar seventeenth-century riddle reads:

Four and twenty white Bulls
sate upon a stall,
forth came the red Bull
and licked them all.

Here the white bulls are the teeth but the red bull is the tongue. With similar imagery, a French riddle describes the tongue and teeth as '*Une vache rouge entourée de veaux blancs*', or 'A red cow surrounded by white calves'.

CHAPTER 11

COUNTING AND ALPHABET RHYMES

CHILDREN LOVE COUNTING and alphabet rhymes. Perhaps it is the predictability that's so appealing: listing letters of the alphabet or numbers makes it easy to know what's coming next and offers a handy way of identifying whose 'turn' it is. Some of the rhymes serve as magic incantations too, used to divine a newborn's future, to foretell fortunes or to predict the kind of person one will marry.

The Alphabet

A Was an Apple Pie

A was an apple pie,
B bit it,
C cut it,
D dealt it,
E eat [ate] it,
F fought for it,
G got it,

H had it,
I inspected it,
J jumped for it,
K kept it,
L longed for it,
M mourned for it,
N nodded at it,
O opened it,
P peeped in it,
Q quartered it,
R ran for it,
S stole it,
T took it,
U upset it,
V viewed it,
W wanted it,
X, Y, Z, and ampersand
All wished for a piece in hand.

This very old rhyme recounts the fate of an apple pie as a means of teaching the alphabet. It was well known as far back as the time of Charles II, who ruled England, Scotland and Ireland from 1660 to 1685. It continued to be popular throughout the following centuries and was used as a vehicle for illustrations by the famous English illustrator Kate Greenaway in her classic children's ABC of 1886, *A Apple Pie.*

A Was an Archer

A was an archer, who shot at a frog,
B was a butcher, and had a great dog.
C was a captain, all covered with lace,
D was a drunkard, and had a red face.
E was an esquire, with pride on his brow,
F was a farmer, and followed the plough.
G was a gamester, who had but ill-luck,
H was a hunter, and hunted a buck.
I was an innkeeper, who loved to carouse,
J was a joiner, and built up a house.
K was King William, once governed this land,
L was a lady, who had a white hand.
M was a miser, and hoarded up gold,
N was a nobleman, gallant and bold.
O was an oyster girl, and went about town,
P was a parson, and wore a black gown.
Q was a queen, who wore a silk slip,
R was a robber, and wanted a whip.
S was a sailor, and spent all he got,
T was a tinker, and mended a pot.
U was an usurer, a miserable elf,
V was a vintner, who drank all himself.
W was a watchman, and guarded the door,
X was expensive, and so became poor.
Y was a youth, that did not love school,
Z was a zany, a poor harmless fool.

Sometimes known as 'Tom Thumb's Alphabet', earlier forms of this rhyme go back to the days of Queen Anne in the early eighteenth century in Britain, while in Boston, Massachusetts, it found its way onto the printed page in *Tom Thumb's Play Book* in 1761. Over the centuries the wording changed until it arrived at the familiar version above.

Numbers

Eeny, Meeny, Miny, Moe

> Eeny, meeny, miny, moe,
> Catch a tiger by the toe.
> If he hollers, let him go,
> Eeny, meeny, miny, moe.

Trying to identify the possible source of this rhyme is like trying to unpick a tangled web. Not least because similar nonsense verses are widely disseminated on both sides of the Atlantic and in non-English-speaking countries.

'Eeny Meeny' is probably the most popular children's counting-out rhyme, used in playground games with groups of children to help decide who is 'it' or who is 'out'. With each word, the speaker points at each child in turn, until only one is left;

that child is then either the 'winner' or out of the game. The version above is the best-known modern form, but other words have sometimes been substituted – 'piggy', 'chicken' or 'tinker' for tiger, for example, or 'screams' or 'wiggles' for 'hollers'. Until relatively recently, the offensive, racist word 'nigger' was generally used instead of 'tiger'.

Given that it is so well known, it is surprising that the rhyme was not familiar to nursery-rhyme collectors in England until relatively late. But it was different across the water: in 1888 the American collector Henry Carrington Bolton recorded a similar verse from Scotland and one from Ireland, and no less than eight comparable rhymes in common use right across the United States.

SPOT THE DIFFERENCE

Variations of this infectious nonsense rhyme have been chanted by children across the world:

- In early nineteenth-century New York:

  Hana, man, mona, mike;
  Barcelona, bona, strike …

- In Germany:

  Ene, tene, mone, mei,
  Pastor, lone, bone, strei …

- In French Canada:

  Meeny, meeny, miney, mo,
  Cache ton poing derrière ton dos …
  [Hide your fist behind your back]

- In Cornish dialect:

  Eena, mena, mona, mite,
  Basca, lora, hora, bite …

I Love Sixpence, Jolly Little Sixpence

I love sixpence, jolly little sixpence,
I love sixpence better than my life;
I spent a penny of it, I lent a penny of it,
And I took fourpence home to my wife.

Oh, my little fourpence, jolly little fourpence,
I love fourpence better than my life;
I spent a penny of it, I lent a penny of it,
And I took twopence home to my wife.

Oh, my little twopence, jolly little twopence,
I love twopence better than my life;
I spent a penny of it, I lent a penny of it,
And I took nothing home to my wife.

Oh, my little nothing, jolly little nothing,
What will nothing buy for my wife?

I have nothing, I spend nothing,
I love nothing better than my wife.

This is the earliest version of the rhyme to appear in print, dating back to the early nineteenth century and the 1810 edition of *Gammer Gurton's Garland*. Later 'jolly sixpence' changes to 'pretty sixpence' and the third line reads: 'I spent a penny of it, I spent another'. But these are just details because the rhyme still works as a process of subtraction, with the number of pennies being reduced by two with each verse until nothing is left; unlike the rhymes that follow, which count *up*, this one counts *down*.

One For Sorrow

One for sorrow,
Two for joy,
Three for a girl,
Four for a boy,
Five for silver,
Six for gold,
Seven for a secret
Never to be told.
Eight for a wish,
Nine for a kiss,
Ten for a bird
You must not miss.

Signs and portents were once thought to be everywhere in nature, and this rhyme details what you could expect if you sighted one, two, three or more magpies. In the Far East, folk belief saw the bird as a symbol of happiness and good luck, but in Europe a magpie – especially a single one – was an ill omen. Because of its constant chattering, it was said to have been ejected from Noah's Ark and had to sit out the Flood perched on the ridge-pole. According to medieval lore, it was the very personification of the Devil himself.

If you are unlucky enough to see a lone magpie, you can mitigate some of the misfortune heading your way by greeting the bird.

Older versions of the rhyme run:

One for sorrow,
Two for mirth,
Three for a wedding,
Four for a death [or birth].

A Scottish variant continues:

Five's a christening,
Six a death,
Seven's heaven,
Eight is hell,
Nine's the De'il his ane sel [the Devil his own self].

One, Two, Buckle My Shoe

One, two,
Buckle my shoe;
Three, four,
Knock at the door;
Five, six,
Pick up sticks;
Seven, eight,
Lay them straight:
Nine, ten,
A big fat hen;
Eleven, twelve,
Dig and delve;
Thirteen, fourteen,
Maids a-courting;
Fifteen, sixteen,
Maids in the kitchen;
Seventeen, eighteen,
Maids in waiting;
Nineteen, twenty,
My plate's empty.

One of those universal rhymes that pop up in different places, this has equivalents in Germany, France, the Netherlands and Turkey. There are plenty of variations on the English wording too

– the counting itself is the point, so in a sense it doesn't matter what words make up the rhyme. *Songs for the Nursery*, from 1805, gives us:

Thirteen, fourteen, draw the curtain,
Fifteen, sixteen, the maid's in the kitchen,
Seventeen, eighteen, she's in waiting,
Nineteen, twenty, my stomach's empty,
Please Ma'am to give me some dinner.

And in *The Counting-out Rhymes of Children*, dated 1888, the American collector Henry Carrington Bolton cited a version that counted up to thirty, and was common in Massachusetts as long ago as 1780.

One, Two, Three, Four, Five

One, two, three, four, five,
Once I caught a fish alive,
Six, seven, eight, nine, ten,
Then I let it go again.

Why did you let it go?
Because it bit my finger so.
Which finger did it bite?
This little finger on my right.

Children have been enjoying this counting-out rhyme for at least two and a half centuries, the first publication being around 1765, in *Mother Goose's Melody*. However, there only the first verse appeared and it was a hare – rather than a fish – that was being caught. The rhyme remained much the same until 1888, when the second verse came into being, based on three American versions in Henry Carrington Bolton's collection (see previous rhyme), to create the rhyme we know now.

Tinker, Tailor

> Tinker,
> Tailor,
> Soldier,
> Sailor,
> Rich man,
> Poor man,
> Beggarman,
> Thief.

Traditionally, children used this rhyme to count cherry stones, buttons, petals, seeds, and so forth, as a form of fortune telling to discover, for example, what kind of person they would marry. It is also used to count out children in a game to ascertain who will be 'it'. Other occupations are often listed instead, such as:

- A captain, a colonel, a cow-boy, a thief (from mid-nineteenth-century England).
- Gentleman, apothecary, ploughboy, thief.
- Rich man, poor man, beggarman, thief, doctor, lawyer, Indian chief (from America).
- Soldier brave, sailor true, skilled physician, Oxford blue, learned lawyer, squire so hale, dashing airman, curate pale.

There are versions in German and Dutch, too, and John le Carré, the famous writer of spy thrillers, chose the first four lines of this rhyme as the title for one of his novels, *Tinker, Tailor, Soldier, Spy* – by deft sleight of hand slipping 'spy' in instead of 'sailor'.

❦

Days of the Week

Monday's Child is Fair of Face

Monday's child is fair of face,
Tuesday's child is full of grace,
Wednesday's child is full of woe,
Thursday's child has far to go,
Friday's child is loving and giving,
Saturday's child works hard for a living,
And the child that is born on the Sabbath day
Is bonny and blithe, and good and gay.

The custom of foretelling a child's personality and future depending on the day on which he or she was born goes back a long way. The English pamphleteer Thomas Nashe recounted how, in 1570s Suffolk, 'yong folks' were told 'what luck eurie one should have by the day of the weeke he was borne on', which suggests that this was a long-held folk practice.

The 'Monday's Child' rhyme, as we know it, was not recorded in print until 1838, in *Traditions of Devonshire*. Even then, there have been numerous variations in the wording, with Christmas Day sometimes substituted for the Sabbath Day (i.e. Sunday) and 'fair and wise' replacing the charming 'bonny and blithe', which is of Scottish origin. *Popular Romances of the West of England*, published in 1872, starts the week with Sunday and gives us the following:

> Sunday's child is full of grace,
> Monday's child is full in the face,
> Tuesday's child is solemn and sad,
> Wednesday's child is merry and glad,
> Thursday's child is inclined to thieving,
> Friday's child is free in giving,
> And Saturday's child works hard for a living.

With so many versions on offer, you really can just take your pick, opting for whichever one most favours the child you have in mind.

Solomon Grundy

Solomon Grundy,
Born on a Monday,
Christened on Tuesday,
Married on Wednesday,
Took ill on Thursday,
Grew worse on Friday,
Died on Saturday,
Buried on Sunday,
That was the end
Of Solomon Grundy.

A whole life lived in the space of one week ... 'Solomon Grundy' was first set down in print by James Orchard Halliwell in *The Nursery Rhymes of England* in 1842, and is a useful vehicle for teaching children the days of the week. Little else is known about it.

Unlike the Johns and Jacks and Toms of other nursery rhymes, 'Solomon Grundy' is such an unusual name that it sounds as if it refers to an actual person – but just who that might be is not known. It's possible that the name is a corruption of 'salmagundi', an English salad dish that originated in the seventeenth century and consisted, typically, of chopped meats and/or fish, anchovies, eggs and vegetables all decoratively arranged together on a plate.

BIBLIOGRAPHY

Key Reading

Opie, Iona and Peter (eds), *The Oxford Dictionary of Nursery Rhymes* (Oxford University Press, 1951). The definitive source for all English-language nursery rhymes.

Other Useful Reading

Alchin, Linda, *The Secret History of Nursery Rhymes* (Nielsen, 2013).

Brewer's Dictionary of Phrase & Fable (Cassell, 1968). A classic work offering explanations of names and phrases used in folklore and mythology.

Dictionary of World Folklore (Larousse, 1995). Excellent background to terms and characters in nursery rhymes and folk and fairy tales.

Jack, Albert, *Pop Goes the Weasel: The Secret Meaning of Nursery Rhymes* (Allen Lane, 2008).

Warner, Marina, *From the Beast to the Blonde* (Chatto & Windus, 1994). Includes a fascinating and authoritative exploration of the Mother Goose figure: Chapter 4, 'Game Old Birds: Gossips III', page 51.

Early Anthologies

Some of the original anthologies of nursery rhymes, referred to earlier in this book, are available second-hand, as reprints or in facsimile digital form. The following are useful sources for finding these anthologies:

AbeBooks
Amazon
Archive.org
Google Books
Forgotten Books
Project Gutenberg
WorldCat

Original titles are also available in the collection of the British Library:

www.bl.uk

INDEX

If you enjoyed *Ring-a-Ring O'Roses,*
you'll love …

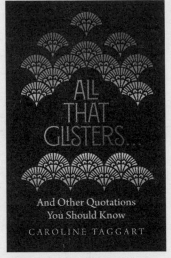

978-1-78243-989-9 in hardback format
978-1-78243-991-2 in ebook format

978-1-78243-997-4 in hardback format
978-1-78929-002-8 in ebook format